ATOMIC ENERGY

ILLUSTRATED WITH DIAGRAMS BY FELIX COOPER
AND WITH PHOTOGRAPHS

HARCOURT, BRACE & WORLD, INC., NEW YORK

ATOMIC ENERGY

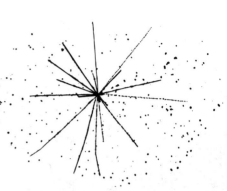

THE STORY OF NUCLEAR SCIENCE
including many home experiments

IRENE D. JAWORSKI
AND ALEXANDER JOSEPH

ISBN 0-15-204438-8

Library of Congress Catalog Card Number: 60-13702
Printed in the United States of America

C.3.70

Acknowledgments

We want to thank those who so generously shared with us their expert knowledge of various aspects of the field of atomic energy. We are especially indebted to Dr. Maurice M. Shapiro, Chief of the Nucleonics Division of the Naval Research Laboratory, and to Dr. R. O. Bondelid of the same division, for their invaluable assistance with the chapters on cosmic rays and accelerators respectively. Dr. Herbert Hauptman, Optics Division of the Naval Research Laboratory, did much to clarify many portions of the manuscript. The personnel of the Educational Services Bureau of the Atomic Energy Commission was most helpful in supplying information, materials, and photographs. We also wish to thank Anita Bickford, Milton Chase, and Dr. Edward C. Wenk for their helpful information and advice, and Dr. Franklin Miller, Jr., for his careful reading of the text.

Irene D. Jaworski
Alexander Joseph

*To Stephen and Catherine and
to Sally, Richard, Janet, and Ellen*

CONTENTS

ATOMIC ENERGY

PART ONE

CHAPTER 1

THE ATOM

When you hear the sharp crack of the bat against the baseball or feel the impact of a grounder in your glove or get stuck with a pin, you may find it hard to believe that the bat, the ball, and the pin are all made up largely of empty space. But it is true nevertheless. Every solid-looking thing in the world is mostly empty space. Such is the fantastic truth about the world we live in.

Everything in the world — living creatures, plants, man-made objects, water, air, the paper of this book you are reading, even the ink that makes up the print — all are composed of atoms, and atoms are mostly empty space.

You have frequently heard that this is the age of the atom. It is. If you were born on December 2, 1942, or later, you were born into the age of the atom, a new kind of age. This is not the same world your parents were born into, or anyone else in the entire history of the world before December 2, 1942, the day that scientists proved they could release the amazing power that is locked within the atom. On that day the atom became for scientists an Aladdin's lamp, ready to provide all sorts of unknown wonders if only they could learn the right way to rub the lamp — that is, the correct techniques to control the behavior of atoms.

In this book you will read about the nature and structure of the atom, the way its various parts behave, and how man has learned to tap this remarkable source of energy. To help you understand the behavior of the atom, there are experiments for you to do at home, which will enable you to see the effects of atoms in action.

Some experiments are extremely simple, involving the use of everyday objects you already have. Others are more advanced and require the purchase of special materials.

WHAT ARE ATOMS?

The word *atom* comes from the Greek word meaning *indivisible* or *uncuttable*. In the fifth century B.C., the ancient Greek philosopher Democritus first proposed the theory that atoms were the basic building blocks of the universe, the very smallest possible bits of matter into which any substance could be broken down. For centuries men knew of nothing smaller than the atom. Today we know that within the tiny atom there are even tinier particles of matter. *Matter* is something that occupies space and has weight. Atoms, although very tiny, do have size and weight, as do the smaller particles within them.

Look at an ordinary steel pin. It is made largely of iron, one of the elements found in nature. The iron atoms are so small that, if you think of a single row of them extending side by side along the length of the pin, there would be about 250 million of them in a pin one inch long. If you take into account the thickness of the pin and include the pinhead as well, you can see that there must be billions of iron atoms in the pin. You know how light the pin feels. It is not surprising then that an individual iron atom weighs only $\dfrac{93}{1,000,000,000,000,000,000,000,000}$ of a gram. There are $28\frac{1}{2}$ grams in an ounce. This bulky fraction can be written another, shorter way: $\dfrac{93}{10^{24}}$.

Scientists use this type of notation for convenience, and we shall use it in this book. Just remember that 10^1 is 10, 10^2 is 100 (or 1 with two zeros), 10^3 is 1,000 (or 1 with three zeros), and so forth. Minus exponents are used to express fractions. For example, 10^{-3} (in which -3 is the exponent) is $\dfrac{1}{1000}$.

Now, what are the iron atoms made of? Since an iron atom is the very tiniest bit of iron possible, when we break it up into its smaller particles, we find bits of matter that can no longer be called iron. The iron atom has a definite number of these smaller particles, as you will see shortly. Let us see now what kinds of particles are found in atoms.

INSIDE THE ATOM

Small as an atom is, it is largely empty space. In its center is the *nucleus,* made up of a definite number of particles called *protons* and *neutrons,* the number depending upon the kind of atom. Around the nucleus, but relatively far away, whirling in various orbits, are the much lighter-weight *electrons.* Protons have a positive charge, electrons a negative charge, while neutrons, as their name indicates, are neutral. A positive charge has the power to attract a negative charge and repel or push away a positive charge. A negative charge attracts a positive charge and repels a negative charge (Figure 1-1).

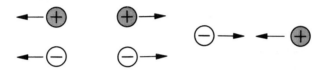

Figure 1-1. Like charges repel. Opposite charges attract.

Now let us try to imagine the structure of an atom. We shall start with the simplest atom of all — hydrogen. The hydrogen atom has only one proton and one electron and no neutron at all. Its structure is shown in Figure 1-2.

Figure 1-2. Hydrogen atom ($_1H^1$).

The word *proton* is the Greek word for *first*. The proton gets its name from the fact that it is the nucleus of the hydrogen atom and hydrogen is the first element. Scientists have arranged the elements in a table according to the number of protons in each element. Hydrogen is the first element because it has one proton. Uranium has 92 protons and is therefore listed as No. 92 in the Table of Elements. You will find this table on pp. 22-23 of this book. It appears in a different form in the Appendix.

In the hydrogen atom the electron travels around the proton in an elliptical orbit. The electron moving around the proton is somewhat like a planet revolving around the sun. In the case of the solar system, however, the force that holds the universe in a definite relationship is called a gravitational force. The forces that hold the parts of the atom in place are electrical.

A diagram cannot show the true distance between the proton and the electron. Although it may seem to us that the parts of such a tiny, invisible thing as an atom must surely be packed closely together, the distance between the nucleus of an atom and the orbit of its electrons is 10,000 times greater than the diameter of the nucleus, as shown in Figure 1-3. Actually, the nucleus occupies only one trillionth (10^{-12}) of the volume of the atom.

Another fact about atoms that a diagram does not reveal is the relative density or weight of the nucleus and the electrons. *Density* of matter refers to how much matter is packed into a given space. Two objects of the same size may differ in density. The denser ob-

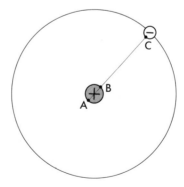

Figure 1-3. An atom is largely empty space. The distance from B to C is 10,000 times greater than the distance from A to B.

ject will be heavier. For example, think of a loaf of bread weighing one pound. Suppose you had a gold brick the same size as the loaf of bread. You know that it would weigh much more than one pound. Gold is much denser than bread. Although a proton and an electron are about the same size, the proton is 1,840 times denser and therefore heavier than the electron. There is no matter anywhere in the universe that is as dense as the nucleus of an atom. It has been estimated that if we could collect one drop of nuclear matter, it would weigh two million tons. You can see now why a diagram cannot give a true picture of the atom and also why we say it consists mainly of empty space.

MAKING MODELS OF ATOMS

The best way to understand the structure of an atom is to build a model of it (Figure 1-4). For this model you will need

modeling clay, preferably of two colors
a piece of thin wire about 14 inches long
a dowel about four to six inches long
a board with a hole in it to hold the dowel
a wire cutter

Make a ball of clay of one color about the size of a marble and mark it with a plus sign. This will represent the positively charged proton. Make another ball of clay, smaller and of a different color, and mark it with a minus sign. This will represent the negatively charged electron. Press the proton onto the top of the dowel. Cut a four-inch piece of wire and pass it through the proton. Take a ten-inch piece of wire, slip the electron onto it, and fashion it into

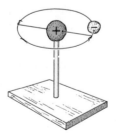

Figure 1-4.   Model of a hydrogen atom ($_1H^1$). When the nucleus is separated from the electron, it is a proton.

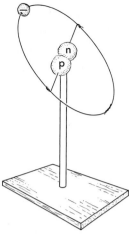

Figure 1-5. Model of a deuterium atom (heavy hydrogen, $_1H^2$). When the nucleus is separated from the electron, it is known as a deuteron.

an ellipse by twisting the ends of the wire together. Attach the ends of the wire crosspiece that runs through the proton to opposite sides of the wire ellipse. You now have the electron in its orbit around the nucleus. This model of a hydrogen atom is more than a trillion times (10^{12}) larger than the real atom. And of course, the model cannot show the actual relationship of the parts; the balls of clay should really be about .0001 inch in size.

You may have heard about another kind of hydrogen called "heavy hydrogen." About one in every 6,500 atoms of hydrogen is heavier than ordinary hydrogen. You can see why it is called heavy hydrogen by building a model of it, as shown in Figure 1-5.

First prepare the parts of the ordinary hydrogen atom. In addition, make an extra proton and an extra electron. Squeeze them together into one ball and mark it zero. The positive and negative charges (plus and minus) combined in this particle cancel out one another, and the particle is called a neutron. In making your model of a heavy hydrogen atom, press the proton and neutron together to make the nucleus and then proceed as before.

Since the nucleus is now twice as heavy as that of the ordinary hydrogen atom, this atom is called heavy hydrogen. Neutrons weigh about the same as protons. The weight of the electron is so small that it is disregarded. Another name for this kind of atom is *deuterium,* from the Greek word meaning *second.* Its nucleus is called a *deuteron* because it has a second particle in it.

You will notice that both kinds of atoms are called hydrogen even though one has a neutron and one hasn't. Both have one proton. It is the *number of protons* that determines the *kind of element.* This number is known as the *atomic number.*

Scientists have a special name for atoms that have the same atomic number but have a different number of neutrons. These are called *isotopes,* from the Greek word meaning *in the same place.* Such elements appear in the same place in the Table of Elements or the Atomic Table. We have not listed the various isotopes as there are so many of them.

In a complete Atomic Table, hydrogen would appear in this form:

$$_1H^{1,2,3}$$

The exponents 1, 2, and 3 represent the three isotopes of hydrogen. You already know the first two kinds of hydrogen. The third isotope of hydrogen, $_1H^3$, has two neutrons and is called *tritium,* meaning *third.* Its nucleus is called a *triton.* You can make a model of a tritium atom by making a second neutron of clay and pressing it together with the other neutron and the proton.

An isotope of a given element may have more or fewer neutrons than the most common isotope of that element. Although the various isotopes of one element have different weights, they all have the same chemical properties. In a later chapter you will read about some of the ways in which various isotopes are used.

The atom next in size to the hydrogen atom is helium, and it is of special interest. Its nucleus, which is called an *alpha particle* when it is separated from its electrons, plays an important role in the story of atomic energy. You can make a model of it by following the diagram in Figure 1-6.

The nucleus contains two protons and two neutrons. Prepare these four balls of clay and squeeze them together to represent the nucleus. This time make two orbits, equal in diameter, and place an electron on each one. Notice that the number of electrons equals the number of protons. This is true of all atoms.

As you squeezed the two clay protons together, did you wonder

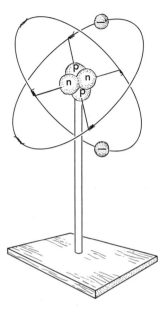

Figure 1-6.   Model of a helium atom ($_2He^4$). When the nucleus is separated from the electrons, it is known as an alpha particle.

why it is that the real protons in the atom remain together instead of repelling each other? It is believed that neutrons are involved in keeping protons within the nucleus, although exactly how this is done remains to be determined. It is significant that every nucleus containing two or more particles has at least one neutron.

When we make models of larger atoms, it becomes too difficult to represent each proton and neutron separately or to give each electron its own orbit. We have to use two short cuts. One is to use one clay ball to represent all the protons and another clay ball, of a different color, to represent all the neutrons. Squeeze these two balls together and mark each half with the correct numbers.

When an atom has more than two electrons, their orbits are not all at the same distance from the nucleus. In the case of the iron atom, for example, its 26 electrons orbit at four different distances from the nucleus. (See Figure 1-7.) As the electrons at a certain distance from the nucleus move about in their individual orbits, their paths create an imaginary hollow sphere, which has been

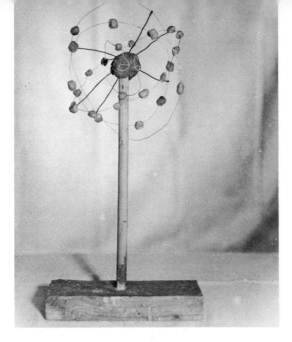

Figure 1-7.   Model of an iron atom ($_{26}Fe^{56}$). Four wire crosspieces of different lengths support the wire ellipses representing the four shells. The figure 26 on the nucleus shows the number of protons.

named a shell. This is not a real or solid shell, merely an area at a certain distance from the nucleus.

In making a model of the iron atom, instead of using 26 separate wire ellipses for the electrons' orbits, it is more convenient to use four ellipses to represent the four shells. Two electrons orbit in the shell closest to the nucleus, known as the K shell. These electrons are called K electrons. At a further distance from the nucleus, eight electrons occupy another shell — the L shell. Beyond this is the M shell, with 14 electrons. The N shell, with two electrons, is the outermost shell.

To represent the four shells of the iron atom, you may use four pieces of wire of different lengths as the crosspieces to support the four wire ellipses, which have different diameters, as shown in Figure 1-7. The ellipses become larger as you move away from the nucleus. First make the K shell and press two electrons onto the wire. Then add the L shell, with eight electrons. Next add the M and N shells, with 14 and 2 electrons.

Remember that the electrons in one shell do not move in a single

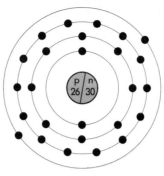

Figure 1-8. Two dimensional diagram of an iron atom ($_{26}Fe^{56}$).

orbit, as the model seems to show. Think of them as whirling in many different orbits, in various planes, but at the same distance from the nucleus.

A two-dimensional diagram of the iron atom can be made as shown in Figure 1-8. The Atomic Table symbols are shown to the right and are explained on page 21.

The model of the helium atom (Figure 1-6) is a complete model. However, both electrons in the helium atom orbit in the same shell. Therefore, a helium atom has only one shell, the K shell. The wire ellipses in the model represent the paths of the electrons, both in the same shell.

The number of electrons and their arrangement in various shells have great significance. It is the number of electrons in an atom that determines its chemical nature. And the composition of the outermost shell determines such matters as whether an element will be a good conducting or insulating material or whether it can combine with other elements to form compounds.

ATOMIC NUMBER AND ATOMIC WEIGHT

In order to understand the structure of different kinds of atoms and to make models of them, you need to know the number of protons, neutrons, and electrons in each kind. This information is supplied by the Atomic Table, which is a basic working tool for any physicist or chemist. Look back at Figure 1-8, the diagram of the iron atom. The figure 26 at the lower left of the symbol is the number of protons in the iron atom. This is called the *atomic number* or *Z number*. The number of electrons in an atom is always the same as the number of protons. Fe in the diagram is the symbol for the element, iron. The *atomic weight* or mass of an atom is concentrated in the nucleus so the atomic weight is the sum of the weights of the protons and neutrons. This figure appears at the upper right of the element symbol. (Each proton or neutron weighs 1 unit.) You find the number of neutrons in any atom by subtracting the number of protons from the atomic weight. In an iron atom, therefore, the number of neutrons is 56 minus 26, or 30.

The symbols in the Atomic Table, from left to right, always represent the following:

$$\underset{\substack{\text{Protons} \\ \text{(Atomic number or Z number)}}}{\overset{\text{Element}}{}} \text{He} \overset{\substack{\text{Protons plus neutrons} \\ \text{(Atomic weight or mass)}}}{}$$

You can check this formula by using the helium atom as an example. In the Atomic Table, helium appears as $_2\text{He}^4$. Subtract the two protons from the atomic weight of four and you get two neutrons, which you know is correct.

Let us take one more example, the uranium atom, an atom that is of great importance in the story of atomic energy. This is listed as No. 92 in the Atomic Table.

$$_{92}\text{U}^{238}$$

From this figure you know that uranium has 92 protons and an atomic weight of 238. To find the number of neutrons, subtract as follows:

atomic weight	238
protons	92
neutrons	146

Like hydrogen and most other elements, uranium has isotopes. Among these, uranium 235 has proved to be the most useful in the production of atomic energy. All forms of uranium have the same number of protons, 92. Remember that it is the *number of protons* that determines the *kind of element*. Uranium 235 has three neutrons less than uranium 238.

Now you should be able to interpret the Atomic Table.

ATOMIC TABLE

This Atomic Table lists the elements and their symbols and gives the number of electrons in each shell, starting with the K shell. The numbers in parentheses are only approximate atomic weights. In the case of the man-made elements, the atomic weight given is that of the most stable known isotope of the element. The subject of stable and unstable elements is discussed in Chapter 3.

Another kind of atomic table appears as a series of boxes and is called the Periodic Table. (See Appendix C.) From now on we shall use the term Periodic Table instead of Atomic Table.

Element	Element Symbol	Number of Electrons	Element	Element Symbol	Number of Electrons
Hydrogen	$_1H^1$	1	Scandium	$_{21}Sc^{45}$	2,8,9,2
Helium	$_2He^4$	2	Titanium	$_{22}Ti^{48}$	2,8,10,2
Lithium	$_3Li^7$	2,1	Vanadium	$_{23}V^{51}$	2,8,11,2
Beryllium	$_4Be^9$	2,2	Chromium	$_{24}Cr^{52}$	2,8,13,1
Boron	$_5B^{11}$	2,3	Manganese	$_{25}Mn^{55}$	2,8,13,2
Carbon	$_6C^{12}$	2,4	Iron	$_{26}Fe^{56}$	2,8,14,2
Nitrogen	$_7N^{14}$	2,5	Cobalt	$_{27}Co^{59}$	2,8,15,2
Oxygen	$_8O^{16}$	2,6	Nickel	$_{28}Ni^{59}$	2,8,16,2
Fluorine	$_9F^{19}$	2,7	Copper	$_{29}Cu^{64}$	2,8,18,1
Neon	$_{10}Ne^{20}$	2,8	Zinc	$_{30}Zn^{65}$	2,8,18,2
Sodium	$_{11}Na^{23}$	2,8,1	Gallium	$_{31}Ga^{70}$	2,8,18,3
Magnesium	$_{12}Mg^{24}$	2,8,2	Germanium	$_{32}Ge^{73}$	2,8,18,4
Aluminum	$_{13}Al^{27}$	2,8,3	Arsenic	$_{33}As^{75}$	2,8,18,5
Silicon	$_{14}Si^{28}$	2,8,4	Selenium	$_{34}Se^{79}$	2,8,18,6
Phosphorus	$_{15}P^{31}$	2,8,5	Bromine	$_{35}Br^{80}$	2,8,18,7
Sulfur	$_{16}S^{32}$	2,8,6	Krypton	$_{36}Kr^{84}$	2,8,18,8
Chlorine	$_{17}Cl^{35}$	2,8,7	Rubidium	$_{37}Rb^{85}$	2,8,18,8,1
Argon	$_{18}Ar^{40}$	2,8,8	Strontium	$_{38}Sr^{88}$	2,8,18,8,2
Potassium	$_{19}K^{39}$	2,8,8,1	Yttrium	$_{39}Y^{89}$	2,8,18,9,2
Calcium	$_{20}Ca^{40}$	2,8,8,2	Zirconium	$_{40}Zr^{91}$	2,8,18,10,2

Element	Element Symbol	Number of Electrons	Element	Element Symbol	Number of Electrons
Niobium	$_{41}Nb^{93}$	2,8,18,12,1	Wolfram	$_{74}W^{184}$	2,8,18,32,12,2
Molybdenum	$_{42}Mo^{96}$	2,8,18,13,1	Rhenium	$_{75}Re^{186}$	2,8,18,32,13,2
Technetium	$_{43}Tc^{(98)}$	2,8,18,14,1	Osmium	$_{76}Os^{190}$	2,8,18,32,14,2
Ruthenium	$_{44}Ru^{101}$	2,8,18,15,1	Iridium	$_{77}Ir^{192}$	2,8,18,32,15,2
Rhodium	$_{45}Rh^{103}$	2,8,18,16,1	Platinum	$_{78}Pt^{195}$	2,8,18,32,17,1
Palladium	$_{46}Pd^{106}$	2,8,18,18,0	Gold	$_{79}Au^{197}$	2,8,18,32,18,1
Silver	$_{47}Ag^{108}$	2,8,18,18,1	Mercury	$_{80}Hg^{201}$	2,8,18,32,18,2
Cadmium	$_{48}Cd^{112}$	2,8,18,18,2	Thallium	$_{81}Tl^{204}$	2,8,18,32,18,3
Indium	$_{49}In^{115}$	2,8,18,18,3	Lead	$_{82}Pb^{207}$	2,8,18,32,18,4
Tin	$_{50}Sn^{119}$	2,8,18,18,4	Bismuth	$_{83}Bi^{209}$	2,8,18,32,18,5
Antimony	$_{51}Sb^{122}$	2,8,18,18,5	Polonium	$_{84}Po^{(210)}$	2,8,18,32,18,6
Tellurium	$_{52}Te^{128}$	2,8,18,18,6	Astatine	$_{85}At^{(210)}$	2,8,18,32,18,7
Iodine	$_{53}I^{127}$	2,8,18,18,7	Radon	$_{86}Rn^{(222)}$	2,8,18,32,18,8
Xenon	$_{54}Xe^{131}$	2,8,18,18,8	Francium	$_{87}Fr^{(223)}$	2,8,18,32,18,8,1
Cesium	$_{55}Cs^{133}$	2,8,18,18,8,1	Radium	$_{88}Ra^{(226)}$	2,8,18,32,18,8,2
Barium	$_{56}Ba^{137}$	2,8,18,18,8,2	Actinium	$_{89}Ac^{(227)}$	2,8,18,32,18,9,2
Rare Earths	57 - 71		Thorium	$_{90}Th^{232}$	2,8,18,32,18,10,2
Hafnium	$_{72}Hf^{179}$	2,8,18,32,10,2	Protactinium	$_{91}Pa^{(231)}$	2,8,18,32,20,9,2
Tantalum	$_{73}Ta^{181}$	2,8,18,32,11,2	Uranium	$_{92}U^{238}$	2,8,18,32,21,9,2

MAN-MADE ELEMENTS					
Neptunium	$_{93}Np^{(237)}$	2,8,18,32,22,9,2	Californium	$_{98}Cf^{(251)}$	2,8,18,32,28,8,2
Plutonium	$_{94}Pu^{(242)}$	2,8,18,32,23,9,2	Einsteinium	$_{99}Es^{(254)}$	2,8,18,32,29,8,2
Americium	$_{95}Am^{(243)}$	2,8,18,32,24,9,2	Fermium	$_{100}Fm^{(253)}$	2,8,18,32,30,8,2
Curium	$_{96}Cm^{(247)}$	2,8,18,32,25,9,2	Mendelevium	$_{101}Md^{(256)}$	2,8,18,32,31,8,2
Berkelium	$_{97}Bk^{(247)}$	2,8,18,32,27,8,2	Nobelium	$_{102}No^{(254)}$	2,8,18,32,32,8,2

MOLECULES

The smallest bit of any of the elements listed in the Periodic Table is an atom of that element. There are iron atoms, copper atoms, chromium atoms, and so on. But you no doubt realize that besides the elements in the table there are countless other substances or materials that we are all familiar with that are not listed — water, wool, rubber, sugar, salt, oil, and so on. These are not elements but compounds. Their smallest bit consists not of a single atom but of a specific combination of two or more atoms. The smallest bit of a compound is a molecule. Thus, the smallest bit of water is a molecule of water, consisting of two hydrogen atoms and an oxygen atom in chemical combination (H_2O).

Electrons play a vital role in the formation of compounds, those in the outer shell forming the link that joins together the two or more atoms in a given compound. Not all atoms can join with others, only those whose outer shell is incomplete, that is, containing less than eight electrons. The great majority of atoms do have incomplete outer shells and therefore do combine with other atoms to form compounds. Some compounds are extremely complex, containing as many as 100 atoms. However, to illustrate the way in which atoms join, we shall use a simple example involving only two atoms. Common table salt is made up of two elements: sodium and chlorine. Sodium has one electron in its outer shell; chlorine has seven. When these two atoms come together, they share a single outer shell, which now has the maximum number of eight electrons. This does not mean that all compounds result in the formation of complete outer shells. Many atoms share outer shells containing less than eight electrons. But if an atom has eight electrons in its outer shell, it will not combine with any other atom.

ATOMIC ENERGY

You know how you feel when you are full of energy. You feel like doing things. Energy makes things happen. It makes things change or move. Scientists define energy as the ability to perform work. We can more readily understand the idea of energy by thinking of the kinds of energy we are familiar with. Sunlight is one kind of energy — radiant energy. It can do things. It can make the color in painted walls and fabrics fade. It can tan or burn your skin.

Heat is another kind of energy. It can create chemical changes in food. It can melt substances, even metals. It makes us perspire. An automobile engine takes the *chemical energy* stored in gasoline and turns it into the *mechanical energy* of the motor, which in turn makes the automobile move. While the automobile is moving, it has energy that is called *kinetic,* from the Greek word *to move.* You are familiar with electrical energy in the form of electric current that lights your lamps and operates the various electrical appliances in your home.

Now what is *atomic* energy? Strictly speaking, chemical energy is "atomic" because it involves electron shells of atoms. However, by atomic energy we mean *nuclear* energy because it is the nucleus of the atom that has, stored within it, the tremendous energy we usually call atomic. This stored energy becomes available under certain conditions that you will read about later. When certain circumstances interfere with the forces holding the nucleus together, one or more particles escape, traveling at high speed. These moving particles have kinetic energy, as does any moving object. This energy possessed by the particles is "atomic energy." You will see later the kinds of work this atomic or nuclear energy can do.

The kinetic energy of moving atomic particles is measured in terms of electron volts, usually in millions (Mev) and even in billions (Bev). Do not let the term *volt* mislead you into thinking of an electron volt as a unit of electrical energy. A volt is a unit used to measure the amount of *push* given to electric current. It is also used to measure the amount of push received by particles, either in nature or in atom-smashing machines. The particles that escape from a nucleus travel very fast, as if they had been given a strong push. Greater speeds mean greater kinetic energy and more electron volts.

Now that you have become somewhat acquainted with the atom, it is time to do some experiments so that you may observe the behavior of atoms at first hand.

CHAPTER 2

EXPERIMENTING WITH ELECTRONS

Tear off a tiny piece of paper from the corner of a newspaper or a facial tissue. Hold it in the palm of your hand. Now try to pick it up with the tip of a plastic fountain pen or the edge of a plastic comb. Nothing happens. Rub the tip of the plastic object briskly several times against your clothing (woolen materials produce good results) and bring it close to the piece of paper. The piece of paper jumps up and attaches itself to the object. Do you know why? When you rubbed the plastic object against the wool, you actually stripped off some electrons from the plastic. That left the object with a positive charge, since it had lost its normal amount of electrons. When it came near the piece of paper, it pulled some of the electrons in the paper toward itself. Thus, the attractive force between the positive plastic surface and the electrons (negative) on the paper surface was strong enough to lift the paper. After the plastic object regains its normal amount of electrons, it no longer holds the bit of paper, which then drops off.

You cannot see an electron. No one has ever seen one, not even with the most powerful microscope in the world. Although electrons are invisible, they make their presence known to us daily in various ways. You are most familiar with the movement of electrons in the form of electric current. The word *current* comes from the Latin word meaning "to run." When you turn on a radio or TV set, or any electrical appliance, you cause electrons to "run." The electrons that form an electric current — in a copper wire, for instance — come from the outermost shell of the copper atoms.

Since there is only one electron in the outer shell, it is easily dislodged. Certain other materials, such as plastic, are poor conductors of electricity because the outer electrons are less easily dislodged.

When the rubbed object picked up the bit of paper, another form of electricity was demonstrated — *static electricity,* so called from the Latin word meaning "standing" or "stationary." As in the case of the copper wire, only the electrons from the outermost shell are attracted. Static electricity was observed by the ancient Greeks, although they did not know of the existence of electrons. They noticed that when a piece of amber was rubbed with a cloth, the amber had the power of attracting small pieces of parchment or linen. Interestingly enough, the Greek word for amber is *electron,* a word that scientists adopted several thousand years later, in 1891, as the name of the elementary unit of electric charge.

You must at one time or another have experienced static electricity in the form of a small shock as you touched the handle of a car door or some other metal object. Or you may have heard the crackle of static electricity as you combed your hair. There are many interesting and simple experiments you can do to observe the behavior of electrons.

CHARGING BALLOONS

Take a toy balloon, stretch it in length and width to make it easier to inflate, and then blow it up. Rub it vigorously against wool. Now place it against the wall and notice how it stays there for a while. Electrons were stripped from some of the atoms in the woolen material and added to the atoms that make up the rubber of the balloon. (Notice that this is the opposite of what happened to the plastic object.) Thus, the balloon, with extra electrons, received a negative charge. When it was brought into contact with the wall, the excess electrons repelled the electrons on the surface of the wall, pushing them back slightly, leaving the wall surface with a positive charge, which then attracted the negatively charged balloon. In the same way you can make the charged balloon stick to your hand or nose. You can also pick up a small piece of paper with it.

What do you think will happen when two negatively charged balloons are brought into contact? Fasten a piece of thread or

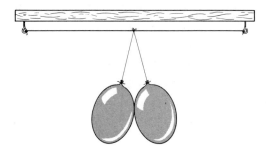

Figure 2-1. Uncharged balloons.

string about a yard long between two points in such a way that it is kept taut. Tie a piece of thread to each of two inflated balloons. Hang the balloons from the same spot in the center of the thread as shown in Figure 2-1. At first they will hang vertically. Next, charge each balloon by rubbing it with wool or fur. Now the balloons repel each other and separate (Figure 2-2).

Next hold the end of a hard rubber comb close to a charged balloon. You will see a slight attraction. Rub the comb with wool. Hold it at its very tip and bring it toward the charged balloon. It is important to keep your hand as far from the balloon as possible because it will attract the balloon. Notice how the charged comb repels the balloon. The comb has a negative charge, the same as the balloon.

Try experimenting with other objects that you have at home. First bring them close to a charged, suspended balloon without charging them. Then charge them and see what happens.

Since you used wool to create a negative charge in the balloon,

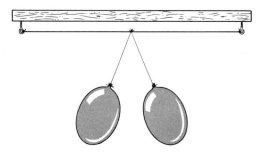

Figure 2-2. Charged balloons repel each other.

the wool lost some of its electrons and therefore, because it is now positively charged, would be expected to attract the balloon very easily. If you rub the balloon with a folded woolen sock and then hold the rubbed part of the sock near the rubbed part of the balloon, you will see a very strong attraction, so strong that you can make the balloon stand straight up in the air by slowly lifting the sock. The wool will hold the balloon in this position until the wool has recaptured its lost electrons.

MAKING AN ELECTROSCOPE

A more sensitive detector of electrical charges is the *electroscope*. As the word indicates, it is a device for "seeing" electrons. That is, it registers their movement. You can make one at home (Figure 2-3) with the following household materials and tools:

a quart milk bottle
a cork for the milk bottle
Corks for small thermos bottles usually fit the quart bottle.
a metal curtain rod with a ball-shaped end, cut to a length of 5″. It is easier to work with the hollow portion. If you use a painted rod, scrape the paint from both ends.
a piece of gummed cellophane tape
a piece of thin aluminum foil, 1¾″ by ¼″
a large nail for making a hole in the cork
a hack saw
a hammer

In the center of the cork make a hole the diameter of the curtain rod by hammering the nail into the cork. With a hack saw cut off a five-inch length of rod, using the part with the ball end. Pass the rod through the cork. It should fit snugly. The ball end projects above the top of the cork about an inch. Hammer down the hollow end of this piece of rod until it is as flat as possible. The flattened end should be as long as the piece of foil. Fasten the foil to the flattened end of the rod with cellophane tape, covering only the top ¼″ of the foil with tape. Carefully lower the rod, cork, and foil into the bottle and twist the cork tightly into place.

Your electroscope is now ready for use. Charge an object by

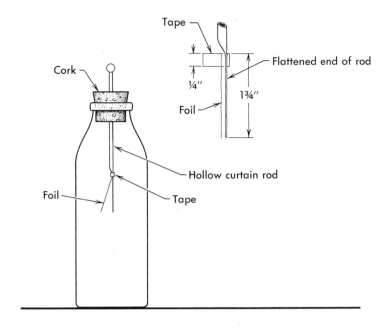

Figure 2-3.   Milk-bottle electroscope.

rubbing it with wool or fur. Touch the rod with the charged object. The lower portion of the foil leaf will move away from the rod because both the rod and the foil receive the same electrical charge and therefore repel each other. The charge is carried through the metal rod in the same way that electric current flows through wires.

If the charge is strong enough, the leaf will remain separated long enough for you to bring an object with an opposite charge to the ball and force the leaf against the rod. If you find that the charge does not last (it varies with the amount of moisture in the air), try this procedure: Touch the tip of the rod with your finger and keep it there to remove any charge that may be on the rod. Bring the charged object near the ball of the electroscope. Remove the finger first and then the object. This should keep the leaf repelled longer.

Another type of electroscope has two foil leaves attached to opposite sides of the flattened end of the rod. When charged, the leaves repel each other.

MAKING AN ELECTROMETER

An electrometer not only shows the presence of a charge but also measures the amount of the electrical charge. To make an electrometer (Figure 2-4), you will need the following materials:

a glass jar with a brass-coated or unpainted screw cap

a very thin double-edged razor blade

a strip of sheet metal several inches longer than the height of the jar and slightly less than $\frac{3}{16}''$ wide. It should fit within the center hole of the razor blade. Metal binding for linoleum may be used or any metal except iron. Instead of the metal strip you may use a large brass paper clip, $3''$ or $4''$ long.

a card to be used as a scale

In the center of the metal strip make a double bend, with two right angles, as shown. The horizontal portion should be no longer than $\frac{1}{4}$ inch. Slip the metal strip through the center hole of the razor blade to the point where the blade will rest in an up and down position on the horizontal part of the strip. Bend the bottom

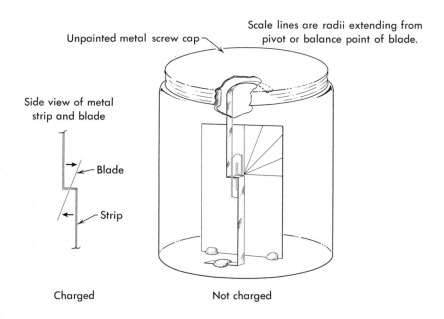

Figure 2-4.   *Homemade electrometer.*

of the strip so that it will stand on the bottom of the jar. Then bend the top of the strip so that it will press snugly against the cap of the jar. If the metal strip does not remain upright, try anchoring the lower end of it to the bottom of the jar with a bit of modeling clay.

To prepare the scale card, cut a card to fit inside the jar you are using. Draw a vertical line on the card so that this line is directly behind the edge of the razor blade when the card stands in the jar. Find the spot on this vertical line that is directly behind the pivot point of the blade. Mark this point with a dot. Now draw four lines out from the dot, as shown in Figure 2-5. To make the lines equally distant from one another, first draw a line at right angles to the vertical line (Step 1). Then divide the remaining space in half (Step 2). Then divide the two smaller spaces in half (Step 3). Once you have the scale card in the jar in the correct position, screw on the cap.

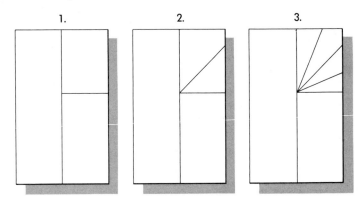

Figure 2-5. Scale card for homemade electrometer.

Follow the same procedure as with the electroscope. As the blade receives a charge, it will move away from the metal strip. You can compare the strength of various charges by noticing to what point in the scale the blade moves in response to various charged objects that are brought in contact with the cap of the jar.

CONTROLLING ELECTRON BEAMS IN YOUR TV

You can have fun with electrons that strike your television screen without damaging the set in any way. For this experiment you will need a strong magnet. If you cannot obtain one, you can make an electromagnet, inexpensively, which will be strong enough (Figure 2-6).

Materials needed

  two pieces of plywood, 2″ by 2″ by ¼″
  a steel bolt ¼″ in diameter, with a nut to fit
  twenty feet of bell wire
  a 1½ volt dry cell (purchasable in a hardware store)
  a wood drill

Drill a hole through the center of each wooden square large enough to take the steel bolt. Assemble the bolt and the wooden squares as shown in Figure 2-6. Wind the wire around the bolt and attach the ends of it to the terminals of the dry cell.

In the picture tube of your TV set, a stream of electrons is shot in the direction of the glass screen, which is coated on the inside with chemicals that glow when electrons hit them. Governed by magnets, this beam of electrons sweeps rapidly across the screen, creating the horizontal lines that you can see.

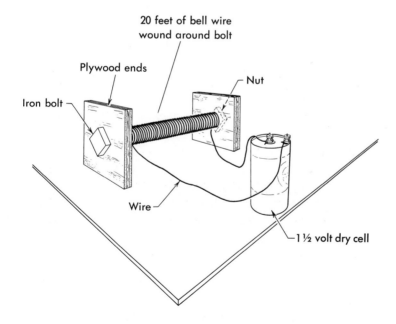

Figure 2-6.   Homemade electromagnet.

With no station being received, but with the set on, bring one end of the magnet near the screen. The lines will move. Now bring the opposite end of the magnet near the screen. The lines will move a different way. Do the same thing with a picture on the screen and notice how you can change the shape of people and objects. If a person is dancing, you can alter his movements.

This experiment shows that moving electrons can be attracted or repelled by magnets. Each electron in the beam has its own magnetic field, which is affected by the magnetic field of the magnet.

PRODUCING AND CONTROLLING ELECTRON BEAMS

You can produce your own electron beams and observe how they are deflected by a strong magnet (Figure 2-7).

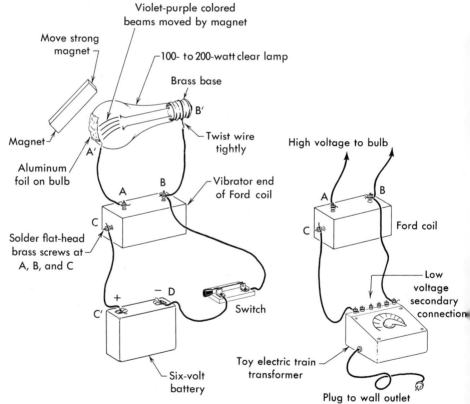

Figure 2-7. Producing electron beams with a battery or transformer as the power source.

Materials needed

a burned-out, clear 100- or 200-watt electric bulb
an induction coil
> The best type can be obtained from a mail-order house for a few dollars. Send for a Model-T Ford ignition coil. Find the number and exact price by looking in the latest catalogue under the heading "Ignition." Or you may be able to find a Model-T Ford ignition coil at an automobile junk yard.

rubber cement
aluminum foil, 1½" square
plastic insulated electric wire
three brass flat-head machine screws, 1" long, $\frac{5}{32}$" thread, with six nuts
single pole, single throw electric switch
six-volt battery, or a toy electric train transformer set to deliver 12 volts
a strong magnet or electromagnet
a soldering kit

Preparing the power supply

Note: This power supply is not dangerous, since it operates from a low-voltage source.

1. Solder flat-head brass screws to the brass terminals of the coil at Points A, B, and C as they appear in Figure 2-7. If you do not know how to solder, you can ask a local radio repairman to do this for you, or perhaps your father or a friend can instruct you. The two top terminals are the high-voltage supply.

2. Connect the coil to a six-volt battery (each connection in this experiment is made by twisting the bared end of the plastic insulated electric wire around the terminal and securing the wire with the nut). Point C on the coil is connected to Point C¹ on the battery, the plus connection. Connect terminal B on the coil to the minus connection of the battery at Point D. Note that terminal B on the coil is near the vibrator end.

3. Break the B-D connection by inserting the electric switch, as shown. Leave the switch open until ready to perform the ex-

periment. In place of the battery you can use an electric train transformer set for 12 volts. This set-up is also shown in Figure 2-7. The transformer operates on alternating current. No switch is needed. You simply pull the plug out of the wall.

Preparing the electron source

1. Cut a piece of aluminum foil 1½ inches square. Scrape off the insulation from the end of a wire, leaving half an inch of wire bare. Wrap one edge of the piece of foil tightly around the bared wire two or three times and cement the foil to the center of the bulb as shown in the diagram at Point A[1].

2. Take another piece of wire and bare enough of it to fit completely around the screw base of the bulb at Point B[1]. Twist the end of the wire around itself to make a tight hold.

3. Connect Point A on the coil with Point A[1] on the bulb.

4. Connect the wire from the base of the Bulb (B[1]) to Point B on the coil.

You are now ready to produce electrons. *Warning:* Do not touch the coil or the bulb while the switch is on or you will get a shock that is not dangerous but still unpleasant. Do not prolong the experiment as some weak X-rays may be produced.

When you turn on the switch, you should see violet-colored beams inside the bulb. Bring a strong magnet near the beams and watch them move. If you reverse the magnet poles, the beams will move in the opposite direction.

X-RAYS

You are of course familiar with some of the uses to which X-rays are put. You may have had an X-ray taken of your teeth or lungs or of some injured part of your body. You know therefore that X-rays can penetrate through the tissue of your body and that they can take a kind of picture.

But you may not know exactly what X-rays are and exactly how they are produced.

How X-rays are produced

At one end of a vacuum tube, like the picture tube of a TV set (a vacuum tube has no air in it), a metal rod (cathode) is connected with a high-voltage source of electricity. This high-voltage current causes the cathode to build up a tremendous negative charge. The electrons crowding on the cathode have no wire to flow through. Instead, they are attracted by a metal plate (anode) with a positive charge at the other end of the tube. The electrons jump across the space and strike the anode. Because these beams of electrons originate in the cathode, they are sometimes known as *cathode rays*. As the electrons strike the atoms of the metal that makes up the anode, they force some of the electrons of that metal to jump out of their shells. When these electrons return to their original shells, energy is released in the form of X-rays. In the case of static electricity only the outermost shell is involved. When X-rays are produced, the inner shells are involved.

In 1895 the German physicist Roentgen, while experimenting with electron beams in an almost airless tube, discovered the presence of X-rays. Because he did not know how they were produced, he named them X-rays. They are also called roentgen rays in his honor. It was not until the early 1900's that scientists determined *how* X-rays were produced. Although Roentgen did not learn that X-rays resulted from electrons jumping back into their shells, he did discover practically all that is known today about the characteristics of X-rays.

Properties of X-rays

X-rays are invisible light rays. Although they cannot be seen, as light can, they behave like light rays. They have a wave length, but much shorter than that of visible light. The following chart will give you some idea of how much shorter they are. In the chart,

Å stands for *angstrom,* a unit of length: $\dfrac{1}{100,000,000}$ of a centimeter (10^{-8} cm.).

Infrared	*Visible light*	*Ultraviolet*	*X-rays*
7,500 Å to .01 cm.	4,000 to 7,500 Å	136 to 4,000 Å	0.1 Å to 135 Å

Like light, X-rays travel at a speed of about 186,000 miles per second (in a vacuum). They can be reflected and refracted and show other reactions similar to those of visible light. Like light rays, they are not affected by electrical or magnetic fields.

Also like light rays, X-rays can darken film. Roentgen was the first person ever to take an X-ray picture. He placed a large iron key on top of a covered photographic plate, which was placed under the tube in which he was directing electron beams at a positively charged plate. When he developed the plate, there was an image of the key on it.

X-rays can do things that visible light rays cannot do. They can knock electrons off the atoms of gases, thus making the atoms positively charged instead of neutral. An atom that has lost one or more electrons is known as a *positive ion* and can attract negatively charged particles. The stray electrons may attach themselves to another atom and create a *negative ion,* which can then attract positively charged particles. An atom is said to be ionized when it loses or gains one or more electrons. The process of losing or gaining electrons is called *ionization.* X-rays can discharge an electroscope by ionizing the atmosphere around it. The ionized air atoms conduct the charge from the electroscope.

You know that X-rays can penetrate body tissue. This penetrating power is used to cure cancer by destroying the malignant cells. Excessive exposure to X-rays is harmful to healthy cells, too. X-rays damage cells by knocking electrons off the atoms of the substances of which the cells are composed, thus causing chemical changes to occur that lead to the death of the cell.

The penetrating power of X-rays is determined by the amount of voltage used to produce the stream of electrons that in turn create the X-rays. Higher voltages produce more penetrating rays, with a shorter wave length. Modern X-ray machines used for medical purposes employ voltages as high as one million volts. Ordinary house current is 110 to 120 volts. Scientists have learned how to increase the speed of the electrons that strike the metal target by accelerating them in a special machine you will read about later. X-rays produced with the aid of such machines can penetrate a yard of steel. The amount of X-ray radiation is measured in units called *roentgens.* A roentgen is the amount of radiation that will produce a certain quantity of ionization in the air.

As X-rays pass through different materials, varying amounts of them are absorbed. That is, X-rays can get through some materials more easily than through others. By studying what proportion of the rays comes through and what proportion is absorbed by a material, scientists can determine what the materials are made of. For example, pigments in oil paintings of unknown origin can be analyzed and the results used to determine the period, the nationality, and sometimes even the identity of the artist.

X-rays provide scientists with an important tool for the discovery of further knowledge about molecules and atoms. Through the use of X-rays, for example, they can determine how the atoms of most solids are arranged and thus study the relationship between the structure of a substance and the properties it possesses. For example, it is interesting to note that a piece of coal and a diamond both consist of carbon atoms. What makes them so different then? The answer is — because their atoms are arranged in a different pattern. You may well wonder how such a fact can be observed when you know that atoms are too small to be seen. This type of knowledge is secured through the science of X-ray crystallography. Most substances are composed of crystals of a substance, which means that their atoms are arranged in definite patterns. In order to study how the atoms are arranged within each crystal of a substance, the crystallographer shoots an X-ray beam through a portion of the substance. Many of the X-rays are deflected and emerge from the crystals in all directions. Some of these strike a photographic plate and create a pattern that reveals the structure of the crystals.

Taking pictures of X-rays

It may surprise you to learn that you have a source of X-rays in your own home: your TV set. In some ways a TV picture tube resembles an X-ray machine. It has a cathode that releases streams of electrons. In fact, TV picture tubes are called *cathode ray tubes*. The cathode is a small cylinder with a chemical coating in the neck of the tube. It is heated by means of a small electric coil and also connected to electric current. The electrons given off by the cathode strike the white coating on the inside of the picture screen. When the electrons strike the screen, they produce a glow that you see assembled into the picture. In addition, as the electrons strike the screen, some of them enter the electron shells of the tungsten atoms, which form part of the coating on the screen, and force electrons to jump out of their shells, thus producing X-rays. You can, without harming your TV set in any way, take a picture of these X-rays. For the best results, use the kind of photographic plate your dentist uses to X-ray teeth. Dental film comes in its own light-proof covering and is sensitive on one side only, as is ordinary film. If you cannot secure dental film from your dentist, you can use fast film, such as Triple X or Royal Pan. You will need to put a sheet of film into a light-proof covering first. You can make a light-proof envelope by folding a piece of black photographic wrapping paper and sealing the open sides with masking tape after you have inserted the film in the dark.

Fasten the film to the TV screen with cellophane tape, with the light-sensitive surface facing the screen. Allow it to be exposed for 10 hours (this does not have to be all at one time) and then develop the film according to the instructions given in the Appendix or have it developed. If you already know how to develop film, you can develop dental film in the usual way.

If you get a picture of the X-rays, you will notice that short lines go off in all directions. These are the paths of X-rays that passed through the film. The TV screen is made up of tiny crystals that point in all directions. If your film remains blank, that shows that your TV set has a lead-glass window that prevents the escape of X-rays.

In this chapter we have nibbled a bit at the outer edge of the atom. Now we shall plunge through the relatively vast space that separates the electrons from their nucleus and begin our exploration of that tiny but marvelous bit of matter — the nucleus of an atom.

CHAPTER 3

NATURAL RADIOACTIVITY

Would you like to take a picture without using any light? If you have a radium watch dial, you can make it take its own picture. Not every dial that glows in the dark contains radium. Some dials have numbers that have been painted with a compound known as "phosphor," which picks up light, stores it, and then glows for several hours in the dark. To tell whether your watch dial contains radium, leave it in the darkness of a drawer for a few days and then take it out in the dark. If it still glows, you will know it contains radium, and you can try the experiment. If not, you can buy a used radium dial inexpensively at a watch-repair shop.

First allow the watch to run down so that the hands are stationary. Remove the rim and the glass. Place the watch face down on a piece of dental X-ray film (or regular film in a light-proof envelope) in a place where they will not be moved out of position. Allow the watch and the film to remain undisturbed for ten days.

After the film is developed, you should see a picture of each number of the dial and of the hands. The numbers will be reversed and appear slightly fuzzy. If you look through the back of the film, you can read them correctly. If the image is faint, the dial does not contain much radium chloride. To get a better picture, allow the watch to remain on the film for three or four weeks.

What created the image on the film? Obviously there was something in the substance of which the numbers and hands were composed that had the power to affect the film emulsion. This energy is called *radioactivity*. Actually, it was through experimenting with film that the French scientist, Antoine Henri Becquerel, discovered the existence of radioactivity in the 1890's. He placed a piece of uranium ore on a light-proof photographic plate and found an outline of the ore after developing the plate. His student, Madame Curie, started to investigate the cause of this strange result. After two years she isolated radium in the uranium ore as the cause of the photographic image. You can easily duplicate Becquerel's historic experiment. You can buy a sample of radioactive ore from a science supply house or hobby shop. Possible types of available ores are: pitchblende and carnotite, containing uranium or radium, and monazite sands, containing radioactive thorium. Most chemistry and mineral sets contain samples of uranium or radium ore. Leave the ore in contact with the film for two weeks.

Since these radioactive substances take their own pictures, such pictures are called radioautographs. More film experiments are given at the end of this chapter.

WHAT IS RADIOACTIVITY?

Most atoms in nature remain unchanged. They keep their original structure, with a fixed number of protons, neutrons, and electrons. They do not give off heat or light or any form of energy. These elements are called *stable*. Almost all the elements we meet in our everyday life are of the stable variety.

Certain atoms, however, are naturally unstable. The best-known are radium, thorium, and uranium. A certain isotope of carbon and a certain isotope of potassium are also radioactive and are of interest because we all have a small amount of each of these isotopes in our bodies. These unstable or radioactive atoms keep breaking down, decaying, disintegrating by emitting radiation, that is, by tossing out particles and rays, a process known as radioactive decay. The terms *radioactive* and *radiation* both come from the Latin word *radius*, meaning "ray." As radioactive atoms shoot out various particles, they are no longer atoms of their original element but become the atoms of other elements. The process of decay continues until all the atoms have become the atoms of an element that is stable, that cannot break down any further. Eventually, uranium, thorium, and radium are converted into lead. Radioactivity in nature is of tremendous importance. Without it, scientists could never have achieved the amazing feat of splitting the atom and utilizing its power.

As the nucleus of a radium atom breaks down, it shoots out alpha particles (helium nuclei), beta particles (electrons), and gamma rays, which are a form of radiant energy similar to light. It is interesting and important to note that the nucleus does not contain alpha particles, beta particles, and gamma rays as such. How then can it emit them? The answer is — and you will understand this statement better after you have read further — that they are created at the time of emission. Even though these particles do not exist inside the nucleus in the form in which they appear during the radioactive process, it is convenient to speak of them as being emitted from the nucleus. These three types of emission or radiation are named after the first three letters of the Greek alphabet: α (alpha), β (beta), and γ (gamma.) Each type has its own special characteristics.

ALPHA PARTICLES OR ALPHA RAYS

As you already know, an alpha particle is a helium nucleus, consisting of two protons and two neutrons. It therefore has a positive charge. At the instant it leaves the nucleus its speed is as high as 8/10ths that of light. Because it interacts with air molecules, it does not travel further than a few inches in air. It is not an especially penetrating particle and can be stopped by a sheet of paper. Since it is electrical, its path can be influenced by the presence of a magnetic field. Since it has a positive charge, it can be attracted by a negatively charged metal plate. Alpha particles have the ability to ionize gases, a very important point to keep in mind as it will help you later to understand how alpha particles can be observed by the use of cloud chambers and Geiger counters. Alpha particles are dangerous to man if they are inhaled or swallowed, or taken into the body through a cut.

When an atom loses an alpha particle, with a loss of two protons, it becomes an atom of another element, with an atomic number two digits smaller than before, and with an atomic weight four digits smaller. Thus radium, with an atomic number of 88

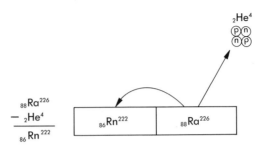

$$\begin{array}{r} _{88}Ra^{226} \\ -\ _{2}He^{4} \\ \hline _{86}Rn^{222} \end{array}$$

Figure 3-1. When a radium atom loses an alpha particle, it becomes a radon atom.

and an atomic weight of 226, with the emission of an alpha particle, in the first step of its decay, becomes radon, with an atomic number of 86 and an atomic weight of 222 (Figure 3-1).

BETA PARTICLES OR BETA RAYS

A beta particle is an electron that is emitted from the nucleus during the radioactive process. Such an emission is known as beta decay. During certain types of decay, a neutron breaks down into a proton and an electron. As an electron (beta particle) is emitted, the remaining proton gives the nucleus one additional positive charge, thus transforming that atom into an atom of an element one number *higher* in the Periodic Table. For example, during the process of radium decay, after the radium atom has emitted three alpha particles (a loss of six protons) and has become an unstable isotope of lead with an atomic number of 82, it emits a beta particle and becomes an isotope of bismuth, with an atomic number of 83. Then it emits another beta particle and becomes an isotope of polonium, with an atomic number of 84. After this, with the emission of an alpha particle, two beta particles, and a final alpha particle, it settles down to a stable form of lead, with an atomic number of 82. Thus, with a loss of five alpha particles (minus 10 protons) and four beta particles, (plus four protons) a radium atom has a net loss of six protons and therefore goes from number

88 to number 82 in the Periodic Table. You can check this result yourself. For every alpha particle lost, subtract two protons. For every beta particle lost, add one proton.

Since beta particles are negative electrical charges, they are repelled by a negatively charged metal plate. They are also bent by magnetic fields but follow a curve that is opposite from the curve followed by alpha particles. They also have the power to ionize gases and to darken film. You can observe them in a cloud chamber and record them with a Geiger counter. Beta particles travel faster than alpha particles and have a greater penetrating power. It takes a sheet of aluminum several millimeters thick (about the thickness of a pie pan) to stop them. They can also produce X-rays.

Every beta particle is accompanied by another particle, discovered only fairly recently, called a *neutrino*, meaning "the little neutral one." It has no electrical charge and, when not in motion, no measurable mass. It is a high energy particle, traveling at a speed about equal to that of light, and can penetrate through several miles of rock.

GAMMA RAYS

Gamma rays may accompany the emission of either alpha or beta particles. They occur when the loss of an alpha particle still leaves the nucleus with an excess of energy that must be removed before the nucleus can become stable. Gamma rays have the same nature as X-rays, only with a shorter wave length and even greater penetrating power. They exist only in motion. When stopped by collision with a particle, they transfer their energy to the particle and cease to exist. Like X-rays, they can injure animal tissue and are used in the treatment of cancer. When people working in atomic plants are shielded against radiation by walls of concrete or lead, it is principally the dangerous gamma radiation from which they are being protected.

Like X-rays, and unlike alpha particles and beta particles, gamma rays are not affected by magnetic fields. Since they carry no charge themselves, they are neither attracted nor repelled by electrical charges. Like X-rays, they travel at the speed of light. In common with X-rays and alpha and beta particles, they can ionize gases and darken film.

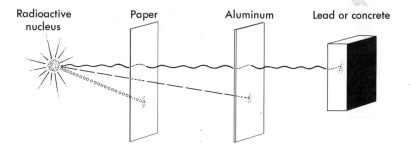

Figure 3-2. Alpha particles are stopped by a sheet of paper, beta particles by a sheet of aluminum. A thick layer of lead or concrete is needed to stop gamma rays.

The diagram in Figure 3-2 shows the relative penetrating power of alpha and beta particles and gamma rays. The chart on p. 47 summarizes the characteristics of the various types of rays mentioned so far.

EFFECTS OF RADIATION

Usually alpha and beta particles do not get inside the body unless a person breathes in or swallows a radioactive isotope that gives them off. Once inside, they are dangerous to health. Gamma rays, being much more penetrating, can pierce the body from outside and are especially harmful. As in the case of X-rays, the ionizing effect of these radiations is one cause of damage to the body. Since the various chemical substances in the body are held together in the form of compounds by means of the sharing of the outer electrons of the combining elements, if electrons are knocked off by the action of alpha or beta particles or gamma rays, the normal body chemistry is disturbed, and ill health, and sometimes death, follows.

The whole story of how radiation affects human life is not yet known. It is believed, however, that one effect is the creation of mutations by the alteration of the genes. The genes are the tiny, submicroscopic bodies in the germ cells that carry inherited characteristics from parent to child. When the structure of the genes has been damaged by radiation, the person or animal involved is not aware of this damage, but his offspring will be different in some way, usually in an undesirable way. Plant growth, too, can be affected by radiation.

CHARACTERISTICS OF RAYS								
Kind of ray	*Nature*	*Attracted by electrically charged plate*	*Deflected by magnetic field*	*Stopped by*	*Speed*	*Can ionize gas*	*Can darken film*
Radioactivity — alpha	positive electrical charge	yes	yes	sheet of paper	up to .8 x 186,000 mi./sec.	yes	yes
beta	negative electrical charge	yes	yes	aluminum (pie plate)	almost as fast as light	yes	yes
gamma	energy Wave-length less than .5 Å	no	no	lead*	of light	yes	yes
X-ray	energy Wave-length from 1 Å to 135 Å	no	no	lead*	of light	yes	yes

Note: Thickness of lead depends upon energy of rays.

RADIOACTIVITY AS A SOURCE OF ENERGY

When a radioactive element decays, it very slowly loses a tiny part of its mass. This loss of mass is converted into energy, according to Einstein's famous formula: $E = mc^2$. *Energy* equals the *amount of mass lost* multiplied by the *speed of light squared.* You can see from this formula that the loss of a very tiny amount of mass produces a tremendous amount of energy, since it is multiplied by the square of the speed of light $(3 \times 10^{10} \text{ cm./sec})^2$. This formula gives the amount of energy in ergs, a unit of energy. You know that speed increases the energy with which an object strikes. If someone threw a bullet at you, it wouldn't hurt much, and it certainly wouldn't penetrate your body. But a bullet shot from a gun tears right through your flesh. This formula explains the fact that the release of all the energy in a given number of atoms of uranium is approximately 55 billion times that of the energy obtained from the burning of the same number of atoms of coal.

This concept of turning mass into energy is the secret of atomic energy.

HALF-LIFE OF RADIOACTIVE ELEMENTS

Radioactivity is not a never-ending process. It lasts only until a radioactive element becomes a stable element. The amount of time it takes a radioactive element to become stable varies tremendously from one element to another. This time is measured by a unit called a *half-life*. Let us illustrate what half-life means by taking radium as an example. This element has a half-life of 1,590 years. After decaying or radiating for 1,590 years, *half* of the atoms in a sample of radium will have become radon. During the next period of 1,590 years, *half of the remaining* radioactive atoms will decay into radon, and so on. You can see that as the amount of radioactive material decreases, the amount of radiation also decreases since it is always a matter of *half of what is left* decaying. See Figure 3-3. A radium atom decays into one radioactive element after another until it finally becomes stable in the form of lead.

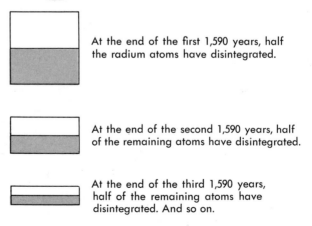

At the end of the first 1,590 years, half the radium atoms have disintegrated.

At the end of the second 1,590 years, half of the remaining atoms have disintegrated.

At the end of the third 1,590 years, half of the remaining atoms have disintegrated. And so on.

Figure 3-3. Radium has a half-life of 1,590 years.

Some elements have a half-life of a few seconds. Others have half-lives of millions of years. The half-life of uranium 238 is 4.5 billion years (4.5 x 10^9). Thorium 232 has the longest half-life: 13 billion years (1.3 x 10^{10}).

Since uranium was present when the earth was formed, it is possible, by determining how much lead has appeared in a given sample of uranium ore, to tell how old that piece of ore is. It has been estimated, using this method, that the earth is five billion years old.

TAKING PICTURES OF RADIOACTIVE MATERIALS

Self-portrait of thorium

You can obtain an interesting radioautograph by using the mantle for a Coleman gasoline lantern. These mantles can be purchased from a large hardware store or from a mail-order house. They are made of asbestos or nylon soaked in thorium oxide. Since the mantles are woven, the radioautograph shows up this pattern.

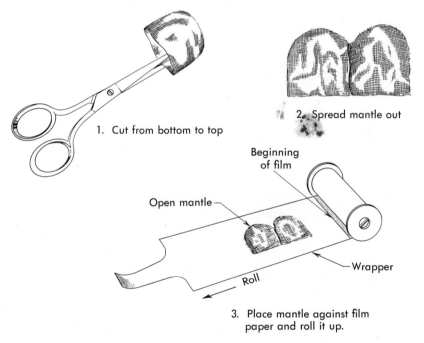

Figure 3-4. Making a radioautograph of a mantle from a Coleman gasoline lantern.

For this experiment you will need a roll of film, such as 120 or 620. First, remove the mantle from the base; then cut along one side of the mantle with a pair of scissors as shown in Figure 3-4. Then open up the mantle to form a flat layer. Working in the dark, unroll the red or green film wrapper until you feel the beginning of the film. Place the mantle on the wrapper right next to the beginning of the film, roll up the film tightly, and fasten the package with cellophane tape. Let the roll stand in darkness for a week. After you develop it, you will see an image of the woven threads of the mantle. As you look at the film, you will see several images. These are the images formed on the layers of film inside the roll. The images on the inner layers of film are fainter because they received less radiation. For the purpose of comparing the different images, you can make prints of each layer or cut up the roll of film into separate pictures.

Radioactive dishes

There are solid-color dishes called "Fiesta Ware" that are manufactured in a variety of colors. One of them is a bright reddish-orange. Strangely enough, the orange glaze is pure uranium oxide. If you can get a plate or a saucer, you can use it for a photographic experiment. The uranium gives off enough beta particles and gamma rays to make a radioautograph of the plate possible if the plate is kept in contact with photographic film for a sufficiently long time.

Allow the dish to rest on a piece of covered film for two weeks. If you have a large plate, allow it to cover only part of the film. This will give you a sharp outline of the edge of the plate. Even though there is enough radiation to secure this effect, it is not harmful to eat food served on these dishes because the radiation is too slight to be dangerous.

Photographing a metal object without light

You can take a picture of a key or any other small metal object by using the orange dish or the thorium mantle. Place the object on a piece of film in a light-proof envelope and cover it with the dish or the mantle. Let them remain undisturbed for two weeks. When the film is developed, you should see a picture of the object. (See Figure 3-5.)

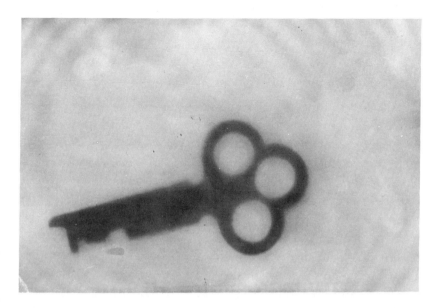

Figure 3-5. The radiation from an orange Fiesta Ware plate produced this picture of a key after one week's exposure. Note the circular lines of the pattern of the plate itself.

PRACTICAL USES OF GAMMA RAY PHOTOGRAPHY

Although alpha and beta rays can affect film, as we have indicated, this is true only at close range, since they do not travel far and are quickly absorbed either in the air or in a material. Gamma rays have much greater penetrating power. Because of this characteristic, they can affect film at some distance from the radioactive source and also pass through metal and other solid materials.

Identifying radioactive ore

Before the days of exploring with a Geiger counter, prospectors used film to determine the presence of radium or uranium ore. When a prospector found rocks that appeared to contain these ores, he would drop unopened rolls of film on the ground in the area and leave them there about seven to ten days. Later, when the film was developed, the telltale tracks of gamma rays would show up on the film if there was any radium or uranium ore in the rocks. You can use a similar procedure to test a rock that you think might contain radioactive ore. Place it on a piece of film in a light-proof envelope and leave it undisturbed for two weeks. Then see if the developed film shows any markings.

Taking pictures of the inside of metallic objects

Several years ago an ocean-depth explorer named Professor Auguste Piccard wished to descend to a great depth under water in a steel diving chamber. Naturally, he wanted to be sure that there was no crack in the hollow steel ball. A piece of radium was placed in the center of the diving chamber, and the entire bell was covered with photographic film in a light-proof covering. The film was left on for several days and then developed. Any crack in the steel, no matter how microscopic, would have allowed gamma rays to pass through the steel. This crack would have appeared as a line on the film. As it happened, there were no cracks, and Professor Piccard used the diving bell to make successful dives to astounding depths in the sea.

In industry the same technique is used to photograph iron and steel castings and to make sure that aircraft engine parts have no invisible cracks.

Protecting workers against dangerous exposure to radiation

Some people work at jobs that expose them to gamma radiation. Workers in atomic energy plants, for example, need to know whether they are absorbing more than a harmless amount of gamma rays. For this purpose they wear film badges, made of dental X-ray film in a special holder. These are developed once a week to determine the amount of radiation to which they have been exposed. The degree to which the film emulsion has been blackened measures the number of milliroentgens (thousandths of roentgens) of radiation.

There is one more kind of radiation that you need to know about before you are equipped to experiment with a cloud chamber or a Geiger counter. It is treated separately because it does not came from radioactive substances as do the kinds of radiation you have been reading about in this chapter. In the next chapter you will read about a kind of radiation that scientists have only recently begun to understand.

CHAPTER 4

MYSTERIOUS RAYS FROM OUTER SPACE

When you charged your milk-bottle electroscope and saw the foil leaf move away from the metal rod, you also must have noticed that it did not stay separated for long but soon collapsed. This same result was noted by physicists who first worked with electroscopes over one hundred and fifty years ago. They observed that the electroscopes never remained charged. The repelled leaf always collapsed, indicating that some outside influence caused the leaf and the rod to lose their original charge.

In trying to determine the nature of this outside influence, scientists at first thought that the electroscope was discharged by radiation from radioactive material in the vicinity of the electroscope. Other scientists, to test this theory, constructed heavy lead chambers capable of stopping all kinds of radiation from nearby radioactive materials. Inside the lead chamber they placed a charged electroscope. In spite of the heavy lead covering, the electroscope discharged. They knew then that they had to search further for the unknown cause of the discharge.

Investigators then took electroscopes up in balloons and found that beyond a certain altitude the higher they went, the more rapidly the electroscopes were discharged. This observation led to the theory that some kinds of unknown radiations were entering the earth's atmosphere from outer space. These radiations were given the name *cosmic rays,* from the Greek word *cosmos,* meaning *universe.*

With the invention of high-altitude balloons and of all sorts of delicate recording equipment, modern scientists have been able to learn a great deal about the nature of cosmic rays — where they come from and how they are distributed throughout the earth's atmosphere. The intensive investigations carried out during the International Geophysical Year, which ended officially in December of 1958, added a great deal to the knowledge of cosmic radiation.

WHERE DO COSMIC RAYS COME FROM? WHAT ARE THEY?

Some of the cosmic rays reaching the earth's atmosphere may originate in the sun, but the great majority are believed to come from outer space. Just as it takes imagination to visualize the invisible world of the atom, it also takes imagination to try to grasp the tremendous distances involved in our galaxy. With its billions of stars, our galaxy is so vast that the cosmic rays that caused your electroscope to discharge may well have been traveling for millions of years, having started out that long ago from outer space.

What started them on their fantastic journey? It is believed today that while some cosmic rays are given off when atoms of the sun break up, most rays are created by the explosion of a star.

Let us follow some cosmic rays in their journey from outer space to earth. As a star explodes, it glows with a great brilliance and sends out particles from its disintegrating atoms. We have no way of knowing at present exactly what kinds of particles are shot out from the exploding stars, since we cannot study such distant portions of the universe. But scientists *have* been able to determine exactly what types of particles reach the earth's atmosphere. By means of sending up recording equipment in plastic balloons to a height of 100,000 feet, they learned that at this altitude cosmic ray particles fall upon the earth's atmosphere at the rate of 20 per square cm. per minute and consist of the following:

    85 per cent are protons (hydrogen nuclei)
    15 per cent are the nuclei of other elements
        Of this 15 per cent:
            90 per cent are alpha particles (helium nuclei)
            10 per cent are nuclei of elements with an atomic number of 26 (iron) or less
  A negligible number of electrons has been observed. We can

guess that originally some nuclei of heavier elements were also present but were broken down into smaller particles during their journey. It is of great interest to scientists to know that cosmic radiation does not include any elements that do not exist on earth. This fact leads to the guess that perhaps all the matter in the universe is made of the same kinds of elements that compose the sun and earth.

Can you picture the explosion of a star with its outpouring of billions upon billions of nuclei? As you know, alpha particles, protons, and other nuclei stripped of their electrons have a positive charge. Because they are electrically charged, they can be affected by magnetic fields when in motion. Scientists have theorized that as these charged particles are flung out from an exploding star, they are whirled around by the magnetic field of their parent star and then flung at high speed into space.

As they travel through space, they meet the magnetic fields of other stars and are made to accelerate even more. Each time they enter a magnetic field, they experience a side push. Each time they get pushed, their speed increases until it approaches the speed of light. Their energy has been estimated at between 100 million and 10 trillion million electron volts, the most likely energy being about 10 billion electron volts.

COSMIC RAYS AND THE EARTH'S MAGNETIC FIELD

The earth's magnetic field has two effects on cosmic rays. It keeps some of them from reaching the earth at all, and it changes the direction of those that do reach earth. Many particles are trapped in the magnetic field. Although they remain in motion, it is a kind of back and forth, spiraling motion, which does not bring them closer to earth. The rays that do reach are bent in such a way that the greatest number of them enter at the earth's magnetic poles, which are near the North and South Poles. The equator receives 90 per cent of the number of rays that the region above the 45th parallel at sea level receives.

COSMIC RAYS AND THE EARTH'S ATMOSPHERE

The particles we described before are those which are observed at very high altitudes, where the earth's atmosphere is extremely thin

— where the number of atoms per cubic foot is about 1 per cent of that found at sea level. These particles are called *primary cosmic rays*. Well above 15 miles from the earth, the particles begin colliding with the atoms of atmospheric gases. When the primary particles strike the nuclei of atoms of gas in the atmosphere, they cause these nuclei to break up. In this process of disintegration two things happen. The nucleus of the atom of gas changes its nature and becomes a nucleus of a different element, as in the process of natural radioactivity. At the same time, a part of the nucleus is smashed into a number of smaller particles, and a shower or burst of particles is emitted as a result of the collision. These particles are known as *secondary* rays. The struck nucleus receives energy from the primary particle and its parts in turn strike other nuclei and create additional secondary rays. It is the secondary rays that actually reach the surface of the earth at the rate of about one per square cm. per minute. It has been estimated that out of 100,000 cosmic rays reaching earth, only one is a primary particle.

NATURE OF SECONDARY RADIATION

If we could only see the commotion caused by the collision between the primary particles (or the secondary particles) and the atoms of gas in the air, it would look something like a Fourth-of-July fireworks display.

The types of particles that are produced by the collisions include practically all the kinds of particles scientists have been able to identify so far. Some of these are already familiar to you: protons, neutrons, electrons, neutrinos, and gamma rays (which have some characteristics of particles). There are several other kinds of particles, which live for only the briefest of moments (less than one millionth of a second). One of these particles is a very tiny one, the same weight as an electron, but with a positive charge. This is called a *positron*. There are several heavier particles, called *mesons,* from the Greek word *mesos,* meaning *middle,* because their weight is between that of the electron and the proton. The weight of the lightest meson is 207 times that of an electron. The heaviest weighs 974 times as much as an electron. There are still heavier particles, heavier than protons, called *hyperons,* from the Greek word meaning *over, above.* Hyperons weigh from about

2,200 to 2,600 times as much as an electron. They are also known as V particles because their presence in a cloud chamber shows up on a photograph as a forked track looking very much like the capital letter V. One leg of the fork is the track of the new nucleus and the other leg is the track of the hyperon. Both mesons and hyperons are found with plus, minus, and neutral charges. (See Appendix B.)

What is the meaning of all these various-sized particles? Simply that the original cosmic particles strike with such force that they smash the nuclei of atoms in the air into an assortment of particles of varying sizes. Even secondary particles retain a tremendous amount of the original energy and go on to smash other nuclei. Eventually, after a series of collisions, the energy of the primary particles has been subdivided among so many particles that these have relatively little energy.

HIGH ENERGY OF COSMIC RAYS

One way to understand the tremendous energy of cosmic rays is to compare them with other forms of radiation in terms of electron volts. The figures given here are *approximate*. Different cosmic ray physicists have made different observations. They probably would not agree on exact limits. However, these figures can give you an idea of how extremely energetic cosmic particles can be.

Alpha particles from radioactive atoms — range from about 4 to 10 Mev (a Mev is a million electron volts).

Beta particles from radioactive atoms — range from fractions of Mev to 15 Mev.

Primary cosmic rays — range from 100 Mev to a trillion(10^{12}) or 10 trillion (10^{13}) Mev. A typical energy is 10,000 Mev.

Secondary cosmic rays — range from fractions of Mev to billions of Mev.

It is because of their energy that cosmic rays are so penetrating. They have been known to pierce a lead block 40 inches thick and have made their way through a quarter of a mile of rock.

EFFECTS OF COSMIC RADIATION

We have already mentioned the fact that cosmic radiation causes the disintegration of atoms in the gases of the atmosphere. In the case of nitrogen, the nitrogen nucleus may become a nucleus of radiocarbon, which is an unstable, radioactive isotope, with a half-life of 5,600 years. The radiocarbon is taken up by plants, which in turn are eaten by animals. When the plant or animal dies, it stops taking in fresh radiocarbon. By measuring the amount of radio-activity produced by the radiocarbon that remains, scientists can tell how long ago the plant or animal lived.

Another power possessed by cosmic rays is the power to strip electrons from atoms (ionization) or to disturb electrons to the point of creating X-rays. The first of these examples has led to a theory that cosmic rays are responsible for evolution. The theory is that by knocking off the electrons from atoms in the genes, cosmic rays have created mutations. Some scientists believe that natural radioactivity has also caused mutations in a similar way.

The creation of X-rays by cosmic radiation is of special interest to the future space traveler. Even if a spaceship is constructed to shield its occupants from direct cosmic radiation, there still remains the problem of shielding them from the X-rays that will be produced when the cosmic particles strike the atoms of the metal of which the spaceship is made.

HOW CAN WE "SEE" COSMIC RAYS?

There are several ways in which secondary cosmic rays can be observed. Their tracks can be seen in a cloud chamber and their presence detected by means of a Geiger counter or a scintillation counter. You will read about these three methods of detecting radiation in the next chapter. The presence of cosmic rays can also be detected by means of an electrometer, and their tracks can be photographed on a special type of film.

Photographing cosmic rays

Scientists make extensive use of film in their study of cosmic rays. A solid block of a special type of sensitive emulsion is made up of many sheets or pellicles, which can later be separated and developed. This block or "film stack," which is sometimes as thick as six inches, is carried to a high altitude by balloon. After the film is developed, the individual layers are pasted side by side to

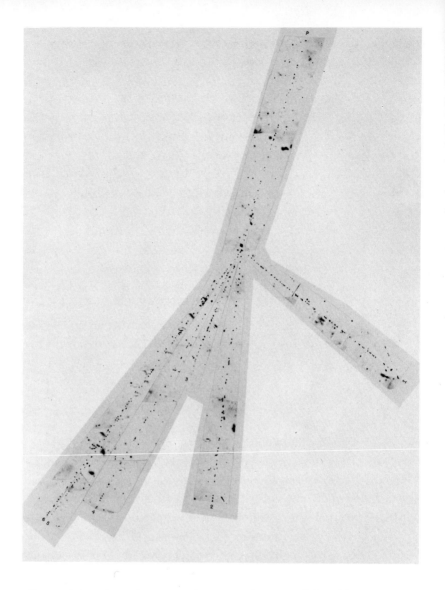

Figure 4-1. Cosmic ray tracks on nuclear emulsion film. A proton (p) has struck another proton in the emulsion, causing it to break up into six particles, which have formed the tracks labeled 1-6. Tracks 5 and 6 have been identified as those of light mesons. (Courtesy of D. T. King, Nathan Seeman, and Maurice M. Shapiro, Naval Research Laboratory)

show the path taken by the cosmic rays as they passed through the layers of film. By examining the thickness and length of the tracks through a special type of microscope, cosmic ray specialists can determine what kinds of particles passed through the film. (See Figure 4-1.)

If you can secure a package of Kodak Nuclear Emulsion film, (to be purchased directly from Eastman Kodak Company, Rochester, N.Y.), you may be able to get a picture of the disintegration of a nucleus by a cosmic particle. To get such a picture, you would have to leave a sheet of film in a light-proof covering for a month in some high place where it would be unlikely to be affected by natural radioactivity from minerals in the ground. The roof of a tall building is a good place to try. It would also be a good idea to enclose the covered film in a water-proof wrapping to protect it from the rain. Develop the film according to the directions supplied with the film. After the film is dried, you will have difficulty in seeing any picture. However, if you examine it under a microscope, you may be rewarded with the sight of a star or burst where an atom disintegrated.

Now that you have become acquainted with the great variety of radiation, you are ready to learn how to build a cloud chamber and a Geiger counter and start using them for the observation of various kinds of rays.

CHAPTER 5

OBSERVING RADIATION

It is possible for you to make even more direct observation of radiation than you can by using film. There are various other devices that are used to detect and measure radiation. Of the six to be described here, three can be duplicated at home. If you make a cloud chamber, you will see the actual paths created by particles. If you make a Geiger counter, you will hear the clicks that are electrically created as particles enter the Geiger tube. The third way is to observe the flashes of light given off by certain chemicals when they are struck by particles. This is the principle of the scintillation counter.

Five of the six devices described in this chapter work on the principle of ionization: the cloud chamber, the bubble chamber, the Geiger counter, the coincidence counter, and the dosimeter. As you read about these devices, notice how the ions are formed and what part they play in making the radiation detectable.

You may recall that the process of ionization was responsible for the natural discharge of your electroscope. The electroscope and electrometer would also be included in any list of detectors operating on the principle of ionization.

THE CLOUD CHAMBER

The cloud chamber was invented in 1912 by C. T. R. Wilson and is often referred to as the Wilson cloud chamber. It is of great value not only in the study of cosmic rays but also in the study of

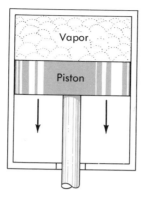

Figure 5-1.   Principle of the Wilson cloud chamber. As the piston moves downward, water vapor or alcohol vapor expands.

what happens when an atom is "smashed" in an "atom-smashing" machine.

It operates on the principle that particles passing through a heavy vapor ionize the vapor's molecules. A particle striking a molecule of water vapor will ionize it into positive and negative ions. The vapor condenses and forms little droplets around the ions and dust particles. These droplets reflect light and thus mark the path of the particle. The resulting track looks like a track from a miniature jet plane or like the smoke track from a plane equipped to do sky-writing. The function of the cloud chamber is to make the vapor that will supply the droplets to mark the path of the particles. Wilson first used water vapor, which condensed when cooled by being expanded suddenly, as shown in the diagram in Figure 5-1. Other, smaller models have a rubber diaphragm instead of a piston. Some cloud chambers use alcohol or a combination of water and alcohol.

USING PROFESSIONAL CLOUD CHAMBERS FOR THE STUDY OF COSMIC RAYS

Physicists use the cloud chamber to study cosmic radiation at ground level and at high altitudes. At ground level they use a giant cloud chamber made of a heavy steel tank with a glass window at the top. A device used to register the arrival of a cosmic ray is called a coincidence counter and is described later in this chapter. It is connected to a mechanism that automatically lowers the piston or releases the diaphragm in the cloud chamber, causing the vapor to expand. This expansion causes the vapor to cool to the point where it is ready to condense. The incoming cosmic particle causes ionization of the vapor molecules, which in turn causes condensation of the vapor, and so the path of the particle is marked. At the same time that the mechanism lowers the piston or releases the diaphragm, it also sets off a photoflood system and puts a motion picture camera into operation so that the track of the incoming particle is photographed. Professional cloud chambers also have an electromagnet that deflects different particles in different ways and aids in their identification. The amount of bending is a clue to the amount of energy.

For high-altitude study of cosmic rays, small cloud chambers are carried to high altitudes by balloons. When the giant clear plastic balloon reaches an altitude of 100,000 feet, the pressure of the helium or hydrogen gas in the plastic bag is so much greater than the almost zero pressure of the atmosphere that the bag bursts. The instruments then descend by parachute. This type of cloud chamber is about 12 by 20 inches in diameter and is operated by a rubber diaphragm. It also functions automatically to photograph incoming particles.

DIFFUSION CLOUD CHAMBER

The type of cloud chamber described so far, known as an *expansion cloud chamber,* is not continuously sensitive. After an expansion of its vapor, it takes about five to ten seconds before the vapor can be compressed and expanded again. Another type of cloud chamber was devised that remains continuously sensitive as long as its vapor source lasts. This type is called a *diffusion cloud chamber.* It consists of a vessel containing air or other gas, which is kept warm at the top and cold at the bottom. A supply of volatile liquid, usually methyl or ethyl alcohol, is placed in a trough near the top. The liquid turns to vapor in the warm region at the top of the container where the vapor pressure is high and keeps drifting or diffusing to the cold region at the bottom of the container where the vapor pressure is low and the vapor condenses. At a certain level the air becomes supersaturated with vapor and the conditions are right for the growth of droplets around ions as in the case of the expansion cloud chamber just after expansion has occurred.

IDENTIFICATION OF PARTICLES

How can physicists tell what kinds of particles made the tracks that appear on the cloud chamber photographs? There are several characteristics of the tracks that help to identify them. The thickness and shape of the track is one clue. Alpha particles make fairly heavy, straight tracks. Protons, having less mass than alpha particles, make a thinner, straight track. Electrons or beta particles make thin, wiggly tracks. If there is a collision between a particle and a nucleus, a distinctive pattern appears. An alpha particle from a radioactive substance may strike the nucleus of a nitrogen atom in the air and produce a forked track. A star or burst of lines indicates that a cosmic particle has disintegrated a nitrogen nucleus.

Another clue to the nature of the incoming particle is the direction in which it is bent by a magnetic field and the amount of bending. Positive particles (alpha particles, protons, positrons, positive mesons) are bent in a direction opposite from that of negative particles (electrons, negative mesons). The greater the energy of the particle, the less it is bent by the magnetic field. Also, more energetic particles make longer tracks.

If a physicist is using a cloud chamber at ground level to study the particles coming from a radioactive source that is placed inside the chamber or held in position outside it, then the direction from which the track is formed is another important clue as to the identity of the particle. If the tracks move out from the radioactive source, then the physicist knows that they are formed by alpha or beta particles and can easily tell them apart by their appearance and degree of bending. If, however, the tracks begin at the top of the chamber and move downward, then he knows they are of cosmic origin. At ground level these are usually mesons. When you use your homemade cloud chamber (see pages 68-69), the direction from which the tracks are formed will be a very important clue for you to take into account.

The cloud chamber can be adapted for the detection of neutrons by the use of a gas that will emit charged particles when struck by neutrons.

CONSTRUCTING A HOMEMADE DIFFUSION CLOUD CHAMBER

At home you can make a diffusion cloud chamber in which you will be able to see the tracks made by alpha and beta particles from a radium watch dial and secondary cosmic particles, usually mesons. If you watch long enough, you may see the forked track produced when an alpha particle strikes a nitrogen nucleus, or you may see several tracks coming from one spot in the chamber where a cosmic particle has struck a nitrogen nucleus. The gamma rays from radium produce electrons, but these tracks are too weak to be seen.

Materials needed

a 12 oz. to one-pint wide-mouthed Thermos bottle and its stopper

a plastic cottage cheese container with the following approximate dimensions: 4″ top diameter, 3″ bottom diameter, 1¾″ deep, no thicker than ⅟₁₆″

three small plastic or wood blocks ¼″ high to be used as spacers

a copper tube 5″ long, outside diameter ½″ to ¾″

soldering iron and solder

a small nail

a disk of sheet copper 2¾″ in diameter (must fit within bottom circumference of plastic container)

flat black paint (small quantity)

blotting paper

a 4″ square of lucite, ⅟₁₆″ to ⅛″ thick (purchased at hobby shop)

gloves

two pounds of Dry Ice (do not touch with bare hands)

one pint of denatured ethyl alcohol or rubbing alcohol

a pure-silk kerchief or tie

a source of light: a focusing flashlight or small projector

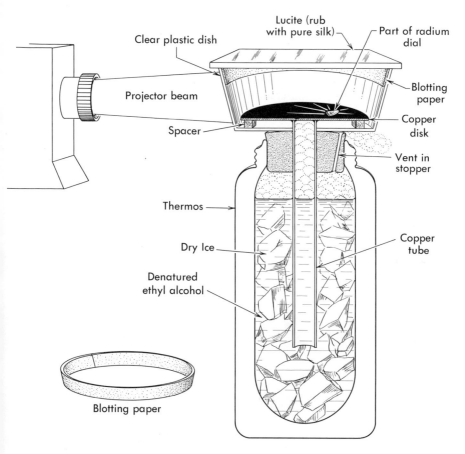

Figure 5-2.   Homemade diffusion cloud chamber.

a radium watch dial (used ones can be purchased cheaply from watch repairmen). *Warning: Do not touch the radium paint with your fingers. Use tweezers.* There are two ways to use the dial. One is to cut out a number. If you wish to use the uncut dial, cover all but one number with a cutout disk of lead foil. If the entire dial is used, there are too many tracks for clear-cut observation.

Making the cloud chamber

1. Heat the copper tube and use it to melt a hole through the center of the bottom of the plastic container. The fit should

be slightly loose. If slight cracks occur in the plastic, they will not affect the operation.

2. Drill or melt a hole through the stopper large enough to permit the insertion of the copper tube. A loose fit is needed to permit the escape of carbon dioxide from the bottle. To insure such venting, use a small nail to punch a hole through the stopper halfway between the center hole and the edge.

3. Solder the copper disk to one end of the copper tube.

4. Paint the top surface of the copper disk with a dull black paint. The black background will make it easier to see tracks.

5. Be certain to use gloves for this operation. Load the Thermos bottle with $\frac{1}{2}''$ pieces of Dry Ice and fill with alcohol. Both ice and alcohol should reach to a height $\frac{1}{2}''$ from where the bottom of the stopper will be. At first the Dry Ice will boil violently. Ventilate the room to carry off the fumes. After a short time the Dry Ice will soften in the alcohol.

6. Cut a strip of blotting paper $\frac{1}{2}''$ wide and long enough to fit snugly within the rim of the plastic container. Dip it into alcohol and place it inside the rim of the container.

7. Place the stopper tightly into position.

8. Place the container on the stopper. Place the spacers on the bottom of the container far enough apart so that they will balance the copper dish in a stable position. Lower the copper tube through the opening and let the copper disk rest on the spacers.

9. Place the lucite cover over the container.

Using the cloud chamber

It is advisable to start with the observation of cosmic rays. Your cloud chamber will work anywhere, but it is better in dry places. First, charge the lucite cover by rubbing it vigorously with silk. The purpose is to clear the field of any stray ions that might interfere with the experiment. In damp weather the plastic top must be charged every 15 minutes or so. The blotting paper strip must be soaked in alcohol every half hour. The Dry Ice and alcohol mixture, however, will last for many hours. Direct the beam of a flashlight or projector into the plastic container as shown in Figure 5-2. Late afternoon sun rays may also be used. You will see thin whitish lines moving downward through the container in the area where the alcohol vapor has condensed. These are the tracks made by secondary cosmic particles, probably mesons. Be patient, as these tracks do not appear continuously.

Once you have become acquainted with the appearance of cosmic ray tracks, you are ready to use your radioactive material. You know that the radium watch dial gives off alpha and beta particles and gamma rays. The alpha particles can be stopped by the wall of the plastic container. If you hold the bit of watch dial *with a pair of tweezers* close to the outside of the container, near the bottom, the beta particles will get through and form thin, threadlike knobby tracks near the bottom of the container. The gamma tracks will not be visible. Although the gamma rays produce photoelectrons, there will not be enough of them to make visible tracks.

Now if you place the bit of dial on the copper plate inside the container, you will see the straight, solid-looking alpha tracks moving out horizontally from the radium source, as shown in Figure 5-3. Actually, alpha particles are sent out in all directions, but they are visible only in the thin layer of vapor at the bottom of the container.

Figure 5-3.   Alpha particles from the piece of radium watch dial produce the horizontal tracks seen in a homemade diffusion cloud chamber.

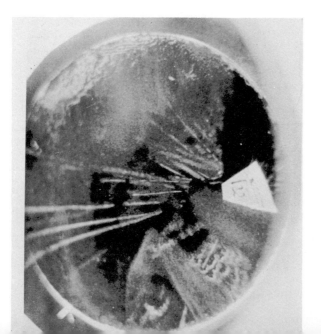

HOW THIS CLOUD CHAMBER WORKS

The purpose of a cloud chamber is to make the path of ions visible. For this, droplets of alcohol are needed. In order to create droplets, vapor must be condensed. What is needed, then, is a big drop in temperature. Copper is a good conductor, lucite a poor one. Thus, the copper tube conducts the heat from the copper disk to the alcohol and the Dry Ice. The lucite cover remains at room temperature. As a result, the temperature difference between the lucite cover and the copper disk is about 150 degrees Fahrenheit or more. The alcohol vapor coming from the blotting paper at the top of the container moves downward because it is heavier than air and passes through this great temperature difference as it approaches the copper disk and condenses.

TAKING PICTURES OF CLOUD CHAMBER TRACKS

You can take pictures of cloud chamber tracks if you have a way of mounting your camera in a steady position. For still pictures you will need a camera with at least an f2.8 lens and a fast film, such as Tri-X. In the dark, aim the camera down into the cloud chamber. Use a time exposure of two to five seconds, and do not allow the beam from your light source to enter the camera lens. The light source should be a slide projector placed three feet away, as shown in Figure 5-2, and the camera·should be at right angles to it. First open the shutter; then turn on the light source. Expose for two to five seconds. Shut off the light and then close the shutter.

For moving pictures use fast black and white film. Take pictures at normal speed using the same light source as for still pictures. Use a camera with an f2.8 lens or with the iris set for f2.8.

THE BUBBLE CHAMBER

The principal use of the bubble chamber is for observing particles that result from atomic collisions caused by bombarding particles from an "atom-smashing" machine. (See Figure 5-4.) It operates on the same principle as the cloud chamber, with one important difference. In a cloud chamber, droplets of moisture condense around the ions in a gas. In a bubble chamber, bubbles of gas form around the ions in a liquid.

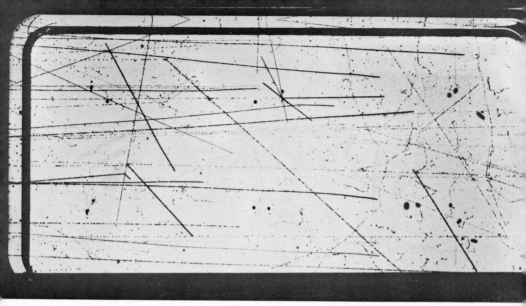

Figure 5-4. Photograph of particle tracks in a propane bubble chamber at the Cosmotron. The heavy tracks stopping in the chamber are protons; the light tracks passing through the chamber were made by mesons. (Brookhaven National Laboratory)

Certain gases, such as hydrogen, nitrogen, propane, and xenon, are used in their liquid state. They are kept in liquid form by means of special refrigerating apparatus. Hydrogen gas, for example, to be converted to a liquid, is cooled to less than 246 degrees below zero (Centigrade), which is its boiling point, that is, the temperature at which the liquid turns to a gas. In a bubble chamber, the liquid gas is allowed to reach a temperature *higher* than its normal boiling point but is prevented from actually boiling by being kept under pressure. In such a state it is said to be "super-heated." With a slight reduction in pressure, the liquid begins to revert to its gaseous state and bubbles are formed around the ions created in the liquid by the incoming particles. Thus the paths of the particles are revealed by the bubble tracks.

Like the expansion cloud chamber, the bubble chamber is not continuously sensitive. After bubbles have formed, there must be an interval of a few seconds during which the original pressure is reapplied to eliminate the bubbles and make the chamber ready for use. However, the bubble chamber is much more sensitive than the cloud chamber. Since liquids are about a thousand times

Figure 5-5. Giant bubble chamber at the Lawrence Radiation Laboratory in Berkeley, California. (University of California)

denser than gases, their atoms are that much closer together. Therefore, an incoming particle produces many more ions for the bubbles to cling to. As a result, bubble chamber tracks supply much more information about particles than do cloud chamber tracks.

Early bubble chambers (the first one was made in 1953) were only a few inches in diameter. The largest one in existence today is the one at the University of California in Berkeley. (See Figure 5-5.) It looks like a bathtub, is six feet long, and holds 150 gallons of liquid hydrogen. It is mounted on a 200-ton electromagnet. The entire device, built at a cost of $2,000,000, is the size of a loco-motive. Particle beams produced by the University of California's powerful atom-smasher, the Bevatron, are piped into the bubble chamber, where their tracks are automatically photographed through a glass window. The photographs of the tracks are then scanned and analyzed by a complex IBM computing machine. Through this method, scientists are able to amass a great quantity of information as to the nuclear events produced by the incoming particles. That is, they have an accurate record of the kinds of disintegrations that have taken place, including information that enables them to identify the various particles that appear in the chamber.

THE GEIGER COUNTER

The well-known Geiger counter, one of several types of ionization chambers, is also known as the Geiger-Müller counter, after its two creators. It is called a counter because it can count the number of particles that strike it.

You can make a Geiger counter at home if you know how to set up a simple electrical circuit. With it you can detect the presence of cosmic rays, beta particles, and gamma rays. Alpha particles cannot penetrate the ordinary Geiger tube and are detected only with a special tube that has a window made of fine mica less than one thousandth of an inch thick. There is another special type of tube that physicists use to detect neutrons. Geiger counters are very widely used: to locate uranium ore, to trace the path of radioactive substances, to measure radiation at high altitudes, and to determine the location of dangerous radioactive powders or liquids that may have escaped from their containers.

HOW A GEIGER COUNTER WORKS

The heart of the Geiger counter is the Geiger tube. This is either a metal cylinder or a metal-lined glass cylinder. In the center of the cylinder is a long thin wire, usually made of tungsten. During manufacture the tube is pumped free of air and filled with a gas at low pressure, such as argon. Two wires lead into the tube. One is connected to the central wire, which has a positive charge. The other is connected to the metal cylinder, which has a negative charge. The voltage is just high enough to charge the space in the cylinder. Thus, an incoming beta particle or gamma ray can create a current that flows from the cylinder to the wire. One beta particle

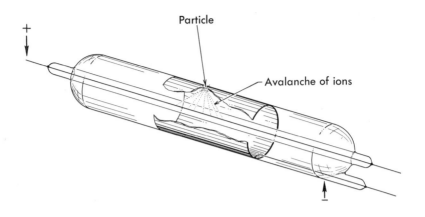

Figure 5-6. Geiger tube. Particle or ray knocks electrons out of gas atoms. These in turn ionize other gas atoms so that a whole avalanche strikes the wire and creates a current.

can dislodge from 10 million to 10 billion electrons. In one millionth of a second, a billion electrons can reach the wire. The positive ions go to the negatively charged cylinder. As the current flows out of the tube through the wire attached to the central wire, it passes through a resistance. This lowers the voltage in the tube so that the current created by a particle is stopped or "quenched," thus making the tube ready to be operated again by the next particle. The current then passes through an amplifier tube somewhat similar to the kind found in hi-fi phonographs and public-address systems. Now it is made strong enough to be heard or seen, depending upon the type of recording device used. The audible type of recorder creates clicking sounds, which can be heard through an earphone. The visible type causes neon bulbs to flash.

Actually, the individual currents produced by the arrival of the particles may occur so rapidly, about 6,000 pulses per second, that it is impossible for the counter to register each one. Therefore, a scaler is used so that a count is made only after a given number of pulses have been received, such as 10, 100, 1,000, etc. One professional counter counts up to 200,000 particles per minute.

You can make a Geiger counter at home using either house current or a battery. Each type can detect cosmic rays, beta particles, and gamma rays.

This unit can be constructed for less than $20, including the cost of the Geiger tube and headphone. It is made with standard radio parts and can be built on a small wooden board in less than an hour. The unit operates from a regular 110-volt A.C. power outlet (which reaches, in each cycle, a momentary peak voltage of about 175 volts). Voltage is doubled by condensers in this circuit to provide just over 300 volts to a low-voltage Geiger tube. *Since most tubes are made to operate at higher voltages, be certain that the Geiger tube you get from your supplier operates at 300 volts.* The supplier of these tubes is Electronic Products, Inc., 11 East Third Street, Mount Vernon, New York.

Materials needed

> one 300-volt Geiger tube
> one headphone
> two 100-milliampere selenium rectifiers (S1 and S2)
> one 0.002-microfarad bypass condenser (C3)
> two 16-microfarad, 300-volt or higher (working voltage) electrolytic condensers (C1 and C2)
> one 1.5-megohm, ¼ watt resistor (R)
> good-quality insulated wire for all connections
> six binding posts; these may be brass screws, one inch long and 6-32 or 8-32 thread, with two nuts each; or Fahnstock clips
> one 4" by 6" wooden board for mounting
> a piece of sheet lead ⅛ inch thick and 4 inches square
> a plastic box or cylinder large enough to enclose entire assembly

Attach the six binding posts to the board as shown in Figure 5-7. Place the two selenium rectifiers on the board at S1 and S2. Note that the plus side of S1 is to the left and the plus side of S2 is to the right. Connect:

> the plus of S1 to the minus of S2
> binding post 2 to the S1-S2 wire
> the plus of S2 to the plus of C2

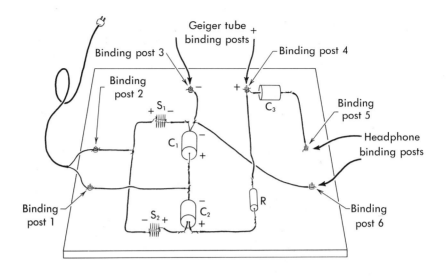

Figure 5-7. Electrical circuit for the homemade Geiger counter operating on alternating current of 110 volts.

the plus of C_1 to the minus of C_2. Note that C_1 has its minus near the top of the board.

binding post 1 to the C_1-C_2 wire

electric wire and plug to posts 1 and 2

the minus of S_1 to the minus of C_1

binding post 3 to the minus of C_1 to binding post 6

the plus of C_2 to either end of R

the other end of R to binding post 4

binding post 4 to one side of C_3

the other side of C_3 to binding post 5

the headphone to posts 5 and 6

Geiger tube plus to binding post 4

Geiger tube minus to binding post 3

To avoid shocks, enclose the entire assembly in a plastic box or cylinder that has a few holes in it to admit radiation. Plug the counter into a 110-volt A.C. power source, and you will be ready to detect radiation. *Warning:* Do not touch any connections or wires while the counter is plugged into power source. You may get a shock.

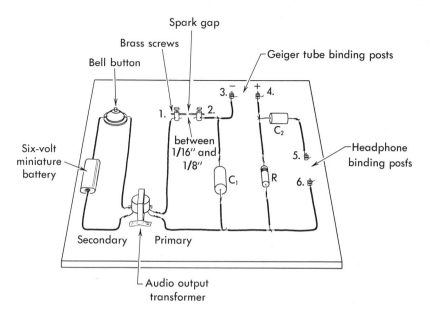

Figure 5-8. Electrical circuit for the homemade Geiger counter operating on six-volt battery.

BATTERY-OPERATED GEIGER COUNTER

This counter has the advantage of being portable. In addition, use of a 700- or 800-volt tube will create greater sensitivity.

Materials needed

    one 300-, 700-, or 800-volt Geiger tube (the 300-volt one is the most expensive)

    one output transformer (from an old radio speaker)

    one 0.25-microfarad 600-volt condenser (C_1)

    one 2-megohm resistor (R)

    two nails, $1\frac{1}{2}''$ long

    one six-volt miniature battery with binding posts or clips

    good-quality insulated wire for all connections

    a bell push button (with screws)

    six binding posts: four may be either 1-inch brass screws of 6-32 or 8-32 thread or Fahnstock clips. The two binding posts for the spark gap must be push-through-hole binding posts (with machine screws).

one 4″ by 6″ wooden board for mounting

a piece of sheet lead ⅛″ thick and large enough to wrap
around the entire cylindrical section of the Geiger tube

one headphone

Assembling the battery counter

Note that in a transformer as used in a radio set, the current usually enters the primary winding and comes out of the secondary
winding. In this construction, the process is reversed. Notice that
in the diagram in Figure 5-8 the current is sent into the secondary
or left-hand side of the transformer, which usually has heavier
wire in this type of transformer.

Attach the bell button to the board with its own screws. Tape
the transformer to the board. Place a small 6-volt battery at the
left. Make the following connections with insulated wire:

one side of the battery to one side of the bell button

the other side of the battery to one secondary connection of
the transformer

the other side of the bell button to the other secondary connection of the transformer.

Prepare the spark gap. Attach push-through-hole binding posts
1 and 2 to the board with machine screws that come up through
the plywood base. Through the horizontal holes in these posts,
place 1½″ nails and fasten them in place by tightening the tips of
the binding posts. The distance between the spark gap points
should be slightly more than 1/16 of an inch. You will see a spark
jump between these two points. The purpose of the spark is to
reduce the voltage for charging the condenser.

Make the remaining connections:

one primary connection of the transformer to binding post 1

the other primary connection of the transformer to one side
of C1 and continue to one side of R and then to binding
post 6

the upper end of C1 to binding post 2 and continue to binding post 3

the upper end of R to binding post 4 and on to one side of C2

the other side of C2 to binding post 5

plus wire (center connection) of Geiger tube to binding post 4

minus of Geiger tube to binding post 3

To avoid shocks, place the assembly inside a plastic box. Make a hole in the box above the place where the Geiger tube is located so radiations can reach the tube directly.

Explanation of battery counter

Each time the bell push button closes and opens the circuit in the left-hand winding of the output transformer, a high voltage is induced in the right-hand winding. This voltage is sufficiently high to jump the spark gap and charge condenser C_1. Repeated opening and closing of the switch builds up the voltage on the condenser. This voltage then appears across the terminal of the Geiger tube. Each time the gas in the tube is ionized by radiation, current flows from the condenser through the resistor (R), where its voltage is made to drop before returning to the plus connection of the tube. The discharge is thereby quenched, and the tube is then ready for the next ionizing radiation. The voltage drop appearing across the resistor at each pulse operates the headphone through a small condenser (C_2).

The momentary-contact switch should be pressed and released sharply about 15 to 20 times. This should charge the condenser sufficiently to have the Geiger tube operate for several minutes. Pressing and releasing at half-minute intervals will maintain the voltage. If the counter fails to operate at first, reverse the battery connections. (The Geiger tube may have been connected in the circuit backwards, depending on the direction of the windings of the transformer.) The counter will give a background count of from 20 to 25 clicks per minute and will respond to relatively low levels of beta and gamma radiation and cosmic rays.

Using the homemade Geiger counter

When you connect your circuit, you will hear clicking sounds. These result from cosmic rays and radiation from radioactive minerals in the rocks and soil in your neighborhood. These clicks are called the background count. Take several counts of the number of clicks per minute to find the average background count.

You can then determine the cosmic ray count by eliminating

the radiation from nearby radioactive sources. If you wrap your Geiger tube with the piece of sheet lead ⅛″ thick, only the cosmic rays will get through.

Now, without the sheet lead, you can try your radioactive source (radium watch dial, thorium mantle, radioactive ore). Place it one half inch from the counter. You will get a strong count, which will consist of the background count plus the gamma and beta counts. To get the total gamma-beta count, subtract the background count.

To determine the beta and gamma counts separately, eliminate the beta count by holding an aluminum pan between the radioactive source and the Geiger tube. Try a second pan to see whether the count drops any further. If it does, you know that one pan did not block all the beta particles. The count you have now is the gamma count plus background. Subtract the background to get the gamma count. To get the beta count, subtract the gamma-background count from the count obtained *without* the aluminum pan.

You can do additional experimenting by measuring the radiation at distances of one inch, two inches, three, etc.

SUMMARY OF GEIGER COUNTER PROCEDURES

Cosmic rays only — cover tube with sheet lead

Cosmic rays and background radioactivity — uncovered tube

Gamma and beta count from your radioactive source — subtract background

Gamma count only — block beta count with aluminum; subtract background

Beta count only — from total of background, beta, and gamma counts, subtract background and gamma counts.

COINCIDENCE COUNTER

You know that the word *coincidence* refers to the occurrence of two events at the same time. A coincidence counter consists of a pair of Geiger tubes arranged in a special circuit. The tubes are arranged so that no current will flow through unless a particle passes through both tubes. Thus they can be set to measure cosmic radiation coming from a definite direction. Sometimes more than two tubes are used to increase the degree of accuracy in determin-

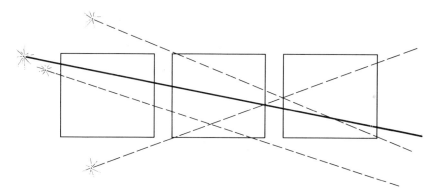

Figure 5-9. *Principle of the coincidence counter. Particles are registered only if they pass through all the Geiger counters.*

ing the direction from which the particle has entered. This type of detector is especially useful in high-altitude cosmic ray research with balloons and rockets. For example, in Figure 5-9, with three counters arranged in a line, only the particle represented by the heavy line will be registered, since it is the only one that passes through all three counters.

POCKET DOSIMETER

The pocket dosimeter, which looks like a fountain pen and is worn by workers exposed to radiation, is a small electrometer with a quartz hair. The dosimeter is so named because it measures the dose or amount of radiation received so that a person can tell when he has reached the maximum degree of safe exposure. The dosimeter records immediate exposure. The film badge records the total amount of exposure over a period of time.

SCINTILLATION COUNTER

Certain substances give off flashes of light or scintillations when they are struck by particles or gamma rays from a radioactive source. Such substances are called scintillators. Radium watch dials produce such scintillations because the dial paint contains radium chloride and a scintillator, zinc sulphide. When the particles or rays from the radium strike the molecules of zinc sulphide, tiny flashes of light are produced. If you rest your eyes for a few minutes in the dark and then look at the radium dial through a 10-power microscope, you will see the scintillations. You do not have to remove the glass.

For about $2.00 you can purchase a device from a science supply house with which to observe scintillations. The device is called a *spinthariscope,* from the Greek word meaning *spark.* It consists of a small tube with a magnifying lens at one end and a bit of radium and a zinc sulphide screen at the other end. The rays from the radium strike the zinc sulphide screen and produce flashes of light.

Extremely weak scintillations, which cannot be seen even with a microscope, can be detected by means of a *scintillation counter.* This device consists of several parts. A scintillator is used to produce the scintillations when it is struck by particles or rays. The scintillator may be a crystal, a plastic, or a liquid usually containing sodium iodide. A special type of electronic tube called an electronmultiplier or photomultiplier magnifies the weak flash of light so that it can be detected and recorded. A scintillation counter can be adapted for the detection of various types of particles and rays, including neutrons, by the use of an appropriate scintillator. Figure 5-10 shows the construction of a scintillation counter in which the phosphor is a crystal or a plastic.

The top of the photomultiplier tube has a tiny plate usually coated with cesium, which is extremely sensitive to light. The particle or ray from the radioactive source strikes the scintillator. From the atoms in the scintillator, tiny flashes of light called scintillations are emitted. The light rays strike the cesium plate and cause the release of electrons. These electrons are then reflected to Plate No. 1. One electron hitting Plate No. 1 can release about 10 electrons. These then bounce off to the next plate, where they are again multiplied by 10. Now at Plate No. 2 there are 100 electrons. These are bounced off to the next plate and so on until each electron emitted from the cesium plate has been multiplied as much as a million times. Now there are enough electrons to produce a measurable current, which flows into an amplifier and is recorded.

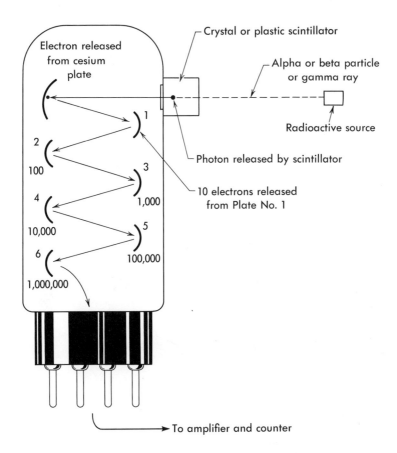

Figure 5-10. Principle of the scintillation counter using solid scintillator or phosphor.

The scintillation counter is regarded as one of the most effective radiation detectors. Since it reacts to even the very weakest kind of radiation, it is much more sensitive than a Geiger counter, particularly in the detection of gamma rays. Because of its very rapid response time, it is very useful in timing fast-moving particles in atom-smashing experiments. Scintillation counters using a liquid scintillator can be made very large. Giant scintillation counters constructed from huge oil drums are used to study cosmic ray showers. There is also a large scintillation counter known as a

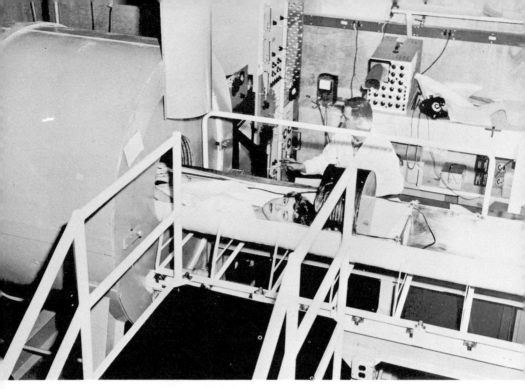

Figure 5-11. A "whole body" scintillation counter. The person whose whole body radioactivity is to be measured is placed inside the counter. The radiations emitted by the body enter a liquid phosphor surrounding the entrance cavity. (Los Alamos Scientific Laboratory)

"whole body counter" because it is made to hold a grown person. (See Figure 5-11.) It is used to measure the total amount of radiation given off by a person's entire body.

PART TWO

CHAPTER 6

SPLITTING THE ATOM

When people speak of atom-splitting or atom-smashing, they really mean nucleus-splitting or nucleus-smashing. The electrons in the outer shells around the nucleus can be easily dislodged by a variety of physical and chemical means. It was the nucleus that proved solid and unbreakable, until it too succumbed to man's never-ceasing efforts to master his environment.

So far in this book we have been referring to the breakup of nuclei only as it occurs in nature: through the decay of naturally radioactive elements such as uranium or radium, and through the collision of cosmic particles with the nuclei of atoms encountered in the atmosphere.

We come now to the crowning achievement of atomic research: man's splitting of the nucleus — the dawn of the nuclear or atomic age. The knowledge of how to break up nuclei opens the door to an unending series of triumphs over the very stuff of which we and everything in the world are made. Now physicists can change one element into another. In addition, they can make stable elements become radioactive. And, as you know, they can release a small portion of the tremendous energy that lies locked within all nuclei.

All scientific discoveries rest upon knowledge previously gained. The achievement of nucleus-splitting rests on a series of developments. Perhaps the most crucial was the discovery of natural radioactivity, for it was as a result of experimenting with the alpha particles from radium that Lord Ernest Rutherford, an English

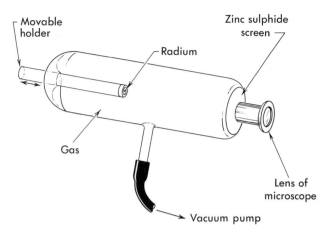

Figure 6-1. Principle of Rutherford's apparatus for observing interaction between alpha particles from radium and nuclei of gases.

physicist, became the first person in history to break up a nucleus. For his contributions to science, he was first knighted and then made a baron.

THE FIRST ATOMIC TRANSMUTATION

Rutherford was engaged in a series of experiments involving the action of alpha particles in various kinds of gases. He filled a vacuum tube with different gases in turn, placed a bit of radium in the tube at the end of a movable holder, and observed through a microscope what happened when the rays struck a zinc sulphide screen.

He was able to move the radium to different positions, to observe how far the alpha particles traveled, and to determine their energy. He had already observed collisions between alpha particles and the nuclei of hydrogen and helium. He knew from watching the flashes on the screen how far the various particles could travel and what their energies were.

One day in 1919, when he had pure nitrogen gas in the tube, something entirely new occurred, something that could not be explained on the basis of ordinary collision. There was a flash on the screen that could not have been produced by an alpha particle. Rutherford concluded that the particle that had reached the screen and had caused the scintillation was a proton that had been

Figure 6-2. *Blackett's photograph of alpha tracks passing through nitrogen gas in a cloud chamber. The forked tracks resulted from the disintegration of two nitrogen nuclei.* (Proceedings of the Royal Society, 1923)

emitted from a disintegrating nitrogen nucleus. In 1925 P. M. S. Blackett, another English physicist, proved that Rutherford's conclusion was correct by photographing alpha tracks passing through nitrogen gas in a Wilson cloud chamber. Blackett took 20,000 photographs, recording 400,000 alpha tracks. Of these tracks, only eight were forked, as in Figure 6-2. As you can see, one of the alpha particle tracks was interrupted and in its place appeared two other tracks, forming a fork. The longer, lighter track was identified as a proton track. The short, stubby track therefore had to be made by the nucleus that remained after the nitrogen nucleus had disintegrated and tossed out a proton.

What was this new nucleus? An alpha particle and a nitrogen nucleus ($_2He^4 + _7N^{14}$) total 9 protons and an atomic mass of 18. Subtract one proton and what do you get? A nucleus with 8 protons and an atomic mass of 17. The mystery nucleus must therefore be an isotope of oxygen, since oxygen has eight protons. There was no doubt that Rutherford had, for the first time in history, changed one element into another. This historic nuclear change is expressed as follows:

$$_2He^4 + _7N^{14} \rightarrow _8O^{17} + _1H^1$$

It so happens that $_8O^{17}$ is a stable isotope of oxygen, making up about $\frac{1}{25}$ of 1 per cent of all the oxygen in nature.

There are two important points to notice about this nuclear change. The number of protons on both sides of the equation adds up to nine. This fact illustrates the principle that when a nuclear change occurs, there is a conservation of charge. That is, electric charge can neither be created nor destroyed. Notice also that the total atomic mass is the same for both sides of the equation, 18 (to the nearest whole number). This fact illustrates the principle of conservation of mass. Mass can neither be created nor destroyed. Sometimes, as you know, there seems to be a loss of mass, as in the case of radioactivity. But the mass has not been destroyed, merely changed into energy. It is also true that energy can be converted into mass. Sometimes this principle is referred to as the conservation of mass-energy.

In order to appreciate what happened in this very first transmutation to be observed, you must realize how tiny the nucleus is in relation to the entire size of the atom. The nucleus occupies one trillionth of the space within the atom and has a diameter estimated to be 10^{-12} cm. Most of the alpha particles — or atomic bullets, as they began to be called — passed right through the nitrogen atoms. It has been estimated that only one alpha particle in 300,000 was able to make a direct hit on the nucleus of a nitrogen atom. In Blackett's experiment, one alpha particle in 50,000 disintegrated a nitrogen nucleus.

We can say that Rutherford's disintegration of the nitrogen nucleus marked the dawn of the nuclear age because it laid the foundation for several vital developments in nuclear physics. In chronological order they are:

    1931 — the first atom-smashing machine
    1932 — the discovery of the neutron
    1934 — the discovery of artificial radioactivity
    1939 — the discovery of fission
    1942 — the first chain reaction, in the first reactor

ATOM-SMASHING

Rutherford and his associates were not content to use only alpha particles from radium as atomic bullets. It was not satisfactory to use a method in which only one particle in many thousands would cause a disintegration. Also, since the alpha particles from radium have energies of only 6 Mev, they cannot split the nuclei of elements containing many protons because of the greater repelling force of such nuclei. Research physicists wanted more effective atomic bullets and so invented machines to speed up a variety of particles and thus give them the energy needed to split more kinds of nuclei. It took almost fifteen years before such machines were designed. You will read about these atom-smashing machines in a later chapter.

DISCOVERY OF THE NEUTRON

Further research with alpha particles from radium led to several discoveries, among them that of the neutron. Sir James Chadwick, an English physicist and an associate of Rutherford's, bombarded beryllium with alpha particles. By a complex process, he determined that the resulting particles were a carbon nucleus and a neutron. Rutherford had guessed a number of years before that the neutron must exist, but no one had been able to prove its existence until Chadwick's work did so in 1932. This change from a beryllium nucleus to a carbon nucleus, with the emission of a neutron, is expressed as follows:

$$_2\text{He}^4 + {}_4\text{Be}^9 \rightarrow {}_6\text{C}^{12} + {}_0\text{n}^1$$

This isotope of carbon is stable and makes up almost 99 per cent of all carbon. Notice again that the number of protons and the atomic mass balance on both sides of the equation.

With the discovery of the neutron, mankind took a giant step toward the mastery of atomic energy.

DISCOVERY OF ARTIFICIAL RADIOACTIVITY

Bombardment of various kinds of nuclei with alpha particles led to another momentous discovery. In 1934, F. Joliot and his wife, Irene Joliot-Curie (the daughter of the famous Marie Curie), were studying the effects of alpha particle bombardment of aluminum. After the aluminum strip had been bombarded for a while, they dissolved it in acid and analyzed it chemically. They found that some of it had become phosphorus. But this isotope of phosphorus was not stable. It had a half-life of 2.5 minutes and was found to toss out positrons, thus becoming a stable isotope of silicon. This sequence of events is expressed as follows:

$$_2\text{He}^4 + {}_{13}\text{Al}^{27} \rightarrow {}_{15}\text{P}^{30} + {}_0\text{n}^1$$
$$_{15}\text{P}^{30} \rightarrow {}_{14}\text{S}^{30} + {}_{+1}\text{e}^0$$

Notice again how the original 15 plus charges and the atomic mass of 31 are all accounted for. The positron, the symbol for which is $_{+1}\text{e}^0$, is a positive electron. The "+1" indicates an electric charge of 1 unit positive. This does not affect the number of protons; it merely indicates the charge of this electron.

The discovery made by the Joliots was important because it revealed the possibility of creating radioactive isotopes. Previous transmutations brought about by alpha particle bombardment had resulted in the creation of new isotopes, but these had all been stable. At least, the scientists working in this field had not become aware of the creation of any radioactive isotopes.

Although the term "artificial radioactivity" is widely used, it is not entirely accurate. It is true that the radioactive isotopes are produced in an artificial manner, but once they have been created, they decay naturally, in their own way A more exact term would be "induced radioactivity."

You will read more about the creation of radioactive isotopes in later chapters, as well as how they are put to use in research, medicine, industry, and agriculture.

DISCOVERY OF FISSION

With the discovery of the neutron, and the knowledge that bombardment by alpha particles could induce radioactivity, physicists lost no time in experimenting with neutron bombardment. In order to secure a beam of neutrons for this purpose, they had to permit alpha particles from radium to strike a substance that would give off neutrons. Enrico Fermi and his associates, working in Rome, were the principal pioneers in this undertaking. Fermi hoped to bombard many elements in the Periodic Table with neutrons and started systematically with hydrogen.

Fermi obtained the neutrons by allowing beryllium powder to be bombarded by the alpha particles from radon, the gas that is formed in the first step of radium decay. He found that neutrons can induce radioactivity in many elements, starting with fluorine and continuing through the Periodic Table.

In the course of these experiments in 1934, Fermi and his helpers made another very important discovery and just missed making a third. He found that "slow" neutrons were much more likely to break up a nucleus than "fast" neutrons. When neutrons are kicked out of a radioactive nucleus, they are traveling at about 10,000 miles per second. Fermi discovered that when these "fast" neutrons passed through paraffin before striking the target, they caused a greatly increased amount of radioactivity in the target element. He reasoned that it was the hydrogen atoms in the paraffin that must have slowed down the neutrons, as moving objects are slowed down best by bumping into objects having the same mass. As you know, a neutron has roughly the same mass as a proton (hydrogen nucleus). You might see for yourself how this rule operates by letting marbles of different sizes collide.

To test his theory, Fermi placed a strip of silver foil and his radon-beryllium neutron source into a goldfish fountain on the grounds of the university where he worked. He observed that the passage of neutrons through the water also resulted in greater radioactivity in the silver target. It is now known that neutrons can be slowed down to a point where they are traveling less than .05 miles per second. For this work in inducing radioactivity through neutron bombardment, and for his discovery of the effects of slowing down neutrons, Fermi received the Nobel Prize in 1938. Shortly thereafter he came to the United States.

It was while Fermi was bombarding uranium with slow neutrons that something new and unusual occurred. It was so strange that Fermi and his associates did not realize what had happened and did not correctly judge the results. Other physicists — Hahn, Strassman, Lise Meitner, the Joliots, Frisch — made similar experiments over a period of several years. They too did not realize what a startling thing had happened. Their tests revealed the presence of radioactive elements, but they did not identify them correctly. Finally, in 1939, Hahn and Strassman, working in Germany, came to the conclusion that the uranium nucleus had tossed out a barium nucleus (No. 56), very far indeed from uranium (No. 92). Since this kind of result had never been known before, Hahn and Strassman published their findings rather hesitantly and consulted Lise Meitner, who, together with Otto Frisch, conferred with Niels Bohr, the Danish physicist. These three worked out a theory that was later verified by experimentation.

The uranium nucleus, having captured a slow neutron, had not become a nearby element with the emission of a particle, as in the case of Rutherford's experience with nitrogen and the Joliots' experience with aluminum. Instead, it had split into two medium-sized nuclei, barium (No. 56) and krypton (No. 36). You will notice that 56 plus 36 equals 92, the number of protons in the uranium nucleus.

Because the split uranium nucleus had divided nearly in half, Lise Meitner named this kind of nuclear disintegration "fission," a term biologists had already coined to describe the way in which one-celled organisms divide when they reproduce. In fact, a schematic drawing of nuclear fission looks very much like a drawing of an amoeba reproducing. Of course, nuclear fission happens much more rapidly.

Later, further knowledge was gained about uranium fission. Natural uranium contains three isotopes: $U238$ (over 99 per cent), $U235$ (.71 per cent), and a very tiny amount of $U234$ that can be disregarded. It is the $U235$ that is fissionable. Occasionally a $U238$ nucleus will fission, but not often enough to matter. In time, more

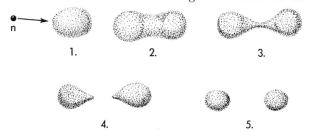

Figure 6-3.   Fission of a uranium nucleus.

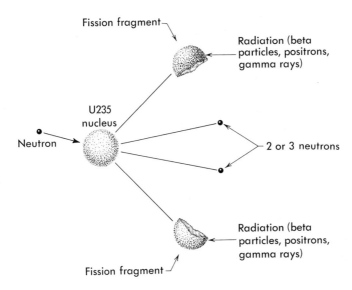

Fission fragment

Radiation (beta particles, positrons, gamma rays)

U235 nucleus

Neutron

2 or 3 neutrons

Radiation (beta particles, positrons, gamma rays)

Fission fragment

Figure 6-4. When a U235 nucleus captures a neutron and splits up, the resulting fission fragments and emitted neutrons weigh about one-fifth of an atomic mass unit less than the incoming neutron plus the U235 nucleus. The mass apparently lost takes the form of the kinetic energy of the emitted neutrons, the fission fragments, and the radiation given off by the fission fragments.

than 60 different kinds of nuclei were found to result from U235 fission, ranging from zinc (No. 30) to gadolinium (No. 64). Counting the additional isotopes resulting from the decay of the radioactive nuclei among the original 60, a total of over 200 isotopes have been identified as resulting from the fission process. Most commonly, the fissioning U235 nucleus breaks into two nuclei that are in the neighborhood of barium and krypton.

Each time a U235 nucleus fissions, there is a tiny loss of mass (equal to one-fifth of a single neutron or proton), which results in the release of about 200 Mev of energy. This energy takes the form of the kinetic energy of the speeding fission fragments and the particles and rays emitted. (See Figure 6-4.) This amount of energy per disintegration of a single nucleus is about 100 times greater than the energy released during the average transmuta-

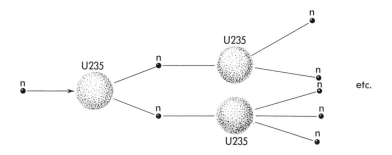

Figure 6-5.   Chain reaction in uranium fission.

tion, in which the new nucleus is only one or two steps away from the original nucleus in the Periodic Table.

Perhaps the most significant fact in the fission of U235 is the emission of neutrons. When a U235 nucleus fissions because it has captured a neutron, it emits an average of 2.5 fast neutrons, which are then available to fission other nuclei and thus keep up a chain reaction, as shown in Figure 6-5. By the sixteenth step, a million neutrons are being emitted at once. Without the extra neutrons there would be no chain reaction, and without a chain reaction there would be no reactors, no atomic power, and no atomic bombs.

THE FIRST REACTOR

The term *reactor* comes from the word *reaction* and serves as a reminder that the operation of a reactor depends upon the chain reaction. The first reactor (Figures 6-6 and 6-7) was constructed at the University of Chicago in 1942 under the supervision of Enrico Fermi, who had already done considerable work at Columbia University on the possibility of producing a chain reaction. It was a secret project, since World War II was going on. Even the name given it — *pile* — was used as a camouflage. A description of this first reactor will illustrate the principle governing the operation of the various types of reactors in use today.

The first reactor was a "pile" of graphite and uranium in the shape of a rough sphere flattened at the top, measuring about 25 feet in each dimension. Graphite, a crystal form of carbon, is the material that is in lead pencils. Layers of graphite bricks into

Figure 6-6.   Artist's drawing of the first reactor, built at the University of Chicago in 1942. (U. S. Army Photograph)

which uranium lumps were inserted were piled up, one layer on the other, until the structure had 57 layers. Layers of plain graphite alternated with layers containing uranium. A wooden framework served as a support. The graphite bricks measured 4⅛ by 4⅛ by 16½ inches and had a total weight of 385 tons. Forty-six tons of extremely pure uranium were used, forty tons in oxide form and six tons in metal form. Several rods made of cadmium and one made of boron-steel were placed into the structure in a horizontal position while the pile was being built. There were both automatic and manual rods. (The automatic rods are safety rods because they fall into place without human control.) Several neutron detectors were placed both inside and outside the pile. These were connected to recording devices and automatic safety

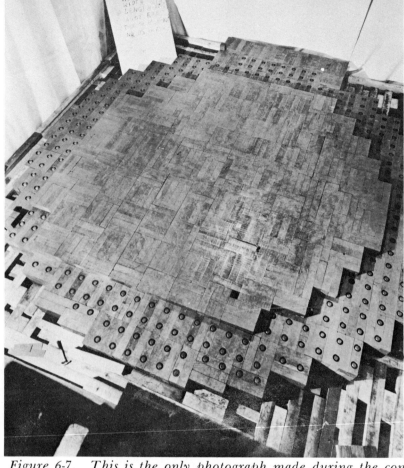

Figure 6-7. This is the only photograph made during the construction of the first nuclear reactor. A plain layer of graphite bricks is in the process of being laid on top of a layer containing uranium slugs. (Argonne National Laboratory)

control mechanisms for moving the rods. As an added precaution, three scientists stood on a platform above the pile, ready to flood it with a cadmium salt solution.

Now what was the reason for the presence of each of these parts? The uranium was there to create and maintain a chain reaction. The fissionable $U235$ would be set off by the stray neutrons that are always around, probably created by the collision of cosmic particles with nuclei in the atmosphere. This part of a reactor, consisting of the fuel, is called the *core*. The graphite was there to slow down the fast neutrons, to make them more effective in causing fission. When fast neutrons from the splitting U235 nuclei hit the graphite nuclei, they bounced off, losing some of their speed and therefore some of their energy. After a number of such collisions, they were slow enough to cause fission. The graphite portion of the reactor is called the *moderator*.

Once a chain reaction started, there had to be some way of controlling it and stopping it. If it had been permitted to go on without any control, it might have created so much heat that the reactor would have been damaged. Also, people present would have been exposed to harmful radiation. The cadmium rods were therefore used to absorb neutrons. They are called control rods. When neutrons strike cadmium nuclei, they are captured without causing disintegration. The boron-steel rod also absorbed neutrons. The amount of fissioning that occurs can be controlled by the position of the rods. With the rods all the way in, the chain reaction does not get started. As the rods are lifted out, the chain reaction begins and increases. It does not reach the point where it can maintain itself until enough uranium is free to interact without interference from the cadmium. The amount of uranium that is sufficient to keep a chain reaction going is described as *critical*. Once the critical size is reached, at least as many neutrons are emitted as are captured. That is, there is at least a one-to-one ratio between captured and emitted neutrons. When the cadmium rods are inserted, the ratio of emitted neutrons drops so that more neutrons are captured than are emitted and so the chain reaction dies out.

The neutron detectors were there to translate into observable data what was going on in the pile: the number of neutrons being produced, which indicated the rate of fission. The neutrons are detected by a special type of Geiger tube that is connected to an amplifier and recording device as in any Geiger counter. As the counter clicks, a recording device draws a graph.

THE FIRST CHAIN REACTION

After a number of pilot model experimental piles had been built and studied, work was begun on the pile that was to produce the first chain reaction. The site chosen was the University of Chicago's squash court, under the west stands of the athletic stadium,

Stagg Field. There, early in November, 1942, the scientists working on the secret project began laying the graphite blocks within a wooden framework. Every other layer contained the uranium slugs. Day by day, layer by layer, the pile grew toward completion. During its construction, the control rods were removed once a day and the amount of fissioning measured by neutron detectors as a clue to how close the reactor was to critical size.

Finally, on December 1, 1942, with the laying of the fifty-seventh layer of graphite and uranium, the pile reached critical size. The next day, December 2, was set for the trial run. On that historic day, the forty-two scientists involved in the project assembled in the squash court, and Fermi gave the signal for the gradual removal of the control rods. Finally, only one rod remained within the pile, but it was sufficient to keep a chain reaction from starting. Then Fermi signaled for the last rod to be moved out a short distance. The counters started clicking; the graph pen began to move upward. Fission had begun. Soon, however, the clicking slowed down; the pen paused in its upward movement. Then the rod was pulled out a little farther, and the same thing happened. Fission took place but died out because not enough neutrons were being produced. The critical amount of uranium had not been permitted to interact. The experiment proceeded in this manner, the control rod being moved out farther and farther.

Suddenly, about half-past eleven in the morning, there was a loud thud. One of the automatic control rods had slammed into position, startling everyone.

"I'm hungry," said Fermi. "Let's go to lunch."

After lunch the trial run proceeded. The spectators watched the dial needle of the counters move, listened to their clicking increase and slow down, and saw the graph pen rise and then level off. One scientist called out the neutron count through a loud-speaker system. Fermi made rapid calculations on his slide rule. He then smiled, closed his slide rule, and said, "The reaction is self-sustaining." The critical size had been reached. It was 3:25 P.M., Chicago time. The group watched the world's first nuclear reactor carry on the first sustained chain reaction in history. The counters clicked faster; the graph pen kept moving up and showed no tendency to level off. Fermi permitted the chain reaction to continue for half an hour. Then he signaled for the control rod to be pushed in. The clicking stopped; the pen slid down across the paper. Those present were aware that a new age had begun. An invisible event, soundless, unfelt, detected only by instruments, had ushered in the nuclear age. Man had unleashed, and then controlled, part of the energy locked within the atom.

WORKING WITH A REACTOR MODEL

With a homemade model of a reactor, a piece of uranium ore, and a Geiger counter, you can have the fun of pretending to operate a nuclear reactor. This model differs from the one Fermi made, described in this chapter, but simulates its operation. Five square pieces of wood are used to make a cube, consisting of four sides and a top. This represents the graphite structure. The outer surface is painted black and marked off into one-inch squares to represent the graphite blocks. The front and back faces of the cube have holes drilled in the center of each square to represent the uranium slugs. A piece of radioactive ore is placed inside the cube, along with a Geiger counter. The "fission" is "controlled" by blocking off the ore from the Geiger counter with lead.

Materials needed

five 12-inch squares of 1″ pine or ¾″ plywood
eight nails, 2″ long for pine, 1″ or 1½″ for plywood
a wood drill
a piece of broomstick about 15 inches long
black and silver paint
a piece of uranium ore
a piece of sheet lead (4″ by 4″) or a pieceof lead pipe 4″ long
    with an inside diameter of one inch (to fit over the end of
    the broomstick)
a Geiger counter with its tube on an extension wire
four flat-head tacks, ½″ long, if sheet lead is used
a block of wood, ½″ x ½″ x ½″

Constructing the "reactor" (See Figure 6-8.)

    1. Prepare the "graphite blocks" by painting the five wooden squares black and marking them off into one-inch squares with

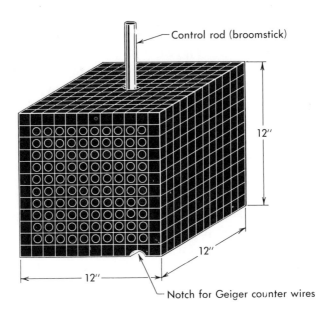

Control rod (broomstick)

12"

12"

12"

Notch for Geiger counter wires

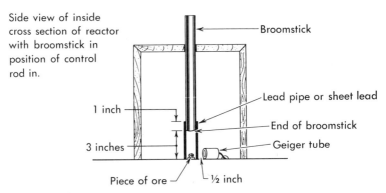

Side view of inside
cross section of reactor
with broomstick in
position of control
rod in.

Broomstick

Lead pipe or sheet lead

1 inch

End of broomstick

3 inches

Geiger tube

Piece of ore

½ inch

Figure 6-8. Construction demonstrating how a graphite-type reactor operates. When the "control rod" is lifted, radiation from the piece of ore makes the Geiger counter click, representing fission.

white chalk. These pieces will be the four faces and top of the "reactor." Drill a hole in the center of each one-inch square on one of the faces. Or, if you prefer, simply draw them on. These holes represent the uranium slugs. At the bottom of this face cut out a notch for the Geiger counter wires to pass through. Assemble the four walls or faces of the "reactor" by nailing them together.

Stand this structure on a table, which will serve as the floor of the "reactor."

2. In the center of the "reactor" top, drill a hole through which to slip the broomstick, which will be the "control rod."

3. Prepare the "control rod" by painting the broomstick silver and fastening either the sheet lead or the lead pipe over the lower end in such a way that it will extend beyond the stick three inches. The sheet lead is wrapped snugly around the broomstick and tacked. The lead pipe is forced on to make a tight fit.

4. In the center of the floor of the "reactor" place the piece of radioactive ore on the small wooden block.

5. Place the Geiger tube on the floor of the "reactor" about half an inch away from the ore. The wires will lead out through the notch to the electrical circuit.

6. Hold the "control rod" in the "in" position by standing it on the floor of the "reactor" in such a way that it covers the ore.

7. Slip the top of the "reactor" over the "control rod" and let it rest on the four walls.

Operating the "reactor"

At first, with the lead covering the ore, the Geiger counter will register only cosmic rays. As you lift up the control rod and start the reactor working, you will hear faster clicking on the counter, because rays from the piece of ore are now registering on the counter. As you cover the ore again, the counts will go down. As you remove the rod, think that now more and more nuclei of $U235$ are splitting and emitting more and more neutrons, which bump into the graphite blocks, slow down, and fission other nuclei. As you replace the rod, think of the neutrons entering the atoms in the control rod and being swallowed up.

CHAPTER 7

NUCLEAR REACTORS

In one of the buildings of the Naval Research Laboratory in Washington, D.C., there is what appears to be a particularly handsome swimming pool. The water in it is of an especially beautiful shade of blue, and very, very clean. The air surrounding the pool is rather warm and moist, the way it usually is in indoor pools. But no one would dream of swimming in this very inviting water because to do so would be to risk death, for the pool is not really a swimming pool at all. It is a nuclear reactor, and the water in it undergoes constant bombardment from deadly neutrons and gamma rays shot out by the fissioning uranium core, which is suspended in the water. (See Figures 7-1 and 7-2.)

This type of reactor doesn't look at all like the one you read about in Chapter 6; yet it follows the same principles and achieves the same results. It is only the materials used in the construction that differ. Since 1942 great progress has been made in the field of nuclear reactors, and many new materials have been found to serve the original purpose. Later, we will give you some idea of the different types of reactors in use today, the kinds of materials of which they are constructed, and their uses. But first it is helpful to know, in some detail, just what goes on in a reactor, in a nuclear sense. That is, what are the atoms doing? What nuclear changes and events are taking place?

WHAT GOES ON IN A REACTOR?

As you know, the intense activity that goes on in a reactor is not

Figure 7-1. This view of the pool reactor at the Naval Research Laboratory in Washington, D. C., shows the core at the bottom of the trusswork attached to the movable bridge. (Official United States Navy Photograph)

apparent, except that you can feel the heat that is generated. You don't hear a sound. For the most part there is nothing to see, either, except that, in the case of the pool reactor, while it is in operation, you can see a weird blue glow in the water immediately surrounding the uranium core. The only other way of determining even part of what is happening is by means of instruments.

The activity that takes place in a reactor is very complex. Many nuclear events happen at the same time, very rapidly — billions of them in a second. In a fissioning uranium core, these are the nuclear happenings: The U235 nuclei change. The U238 nuclei change. Plutonium is produced. A variety of isotopes are created, both stable and radioactive. Neutrons are produced, as well as alpha and beta particles, gamma rays, and positrons. And, as a result of all this activity, great energy is released in the form of heat. Let us consider these happenings singly.

Nuclear changes in U235

When the U235 nuclei capture slow neutrons, they fission, breaking apart into two fragments and emitting an average of 2.5 neutrons per fission. These fission fragments, which occur in 100 or more different combinations of 60 different nuclei, may be either stable or radioactive. The radioactive nuclei in turn give off particles until they become stable. They emit beta particles or positrons, or both, with or without gamma radiation. The fission fragments, though moving rapidly, do not get very far, penetrating about .0005 cm. into the surrounding materials.

Production of neutrons

The fact that U235 nuclei in fissioning emit an average of 2.5 neutrons per fission is, of course, the most important aspect of the fission process, because on it depends the chain reaction. Fission

Figure 7-2.   The face of the Naval Research Laboratory Reactor showing the end of the pool, which terminates in a special radiation shield. (Naval Research Laboratory)

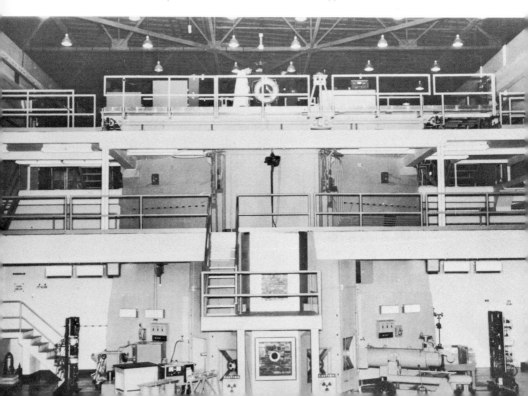

accounts for 99 per cent of all the neutrons produced while a reactor is in operation. The remaining 1 per cent come from unstable nuclei, which have been formed by the delayed decay of fission fragments. These are known as "delayed" neutrons, since they are produced an average of 12 seconds later than the neutrons coming from the fissioning U235 nuclei. The delayed neutrons play a vital role in the control of the chain reaction. Because they occur more slowly than the other neutrons, which appear almost instantaneously, they provide enough time for the control rods to be moved into position to slow down the chain reaction.

Unlike the fission fragments, which have a high positive charge and therefore are easily stopped by the surrounding material, the neutrons, being uncharged, travel more freely through the core. Before they are slowed down by bumping into the nuclei of the moderator, they are "fast" neutrons, traveling at 10,000 miles per second, with a kinetic energy of 2 Mev. Not all of them meet the same fate; not all go on to fission other U235 nuclei. Actually, less than half do so. The diagram in Figure 7-3 shows what might happen to 1000 fast neutrons in a reactor made of ordinary uranium when the control rods are removed.

In addition to being responsible for the chain reaction, neutrons are used for research and for a number of practical purposes, as you will see later in the chapter.

Nuclear changes in U238

Although the U238 itself can fission only very rarely, it can produce a fissionable material — plutonium — when it captures a neutron. This nuclear change happens in several steps, as follows: With the capture of a fast or slow neutron (see Figure 7-3), a nucleus of U238 becomes U239 with emission of a gamma ray. This uranium isotope has a half-life of 23½ minutes. In decaying, it emits a beta particle, $_{-1}e^0$ (a neutron is changed to a proton). The daughter element now has 93 protons and is no longer uranium but a new element that does not exist in nature. It has been named neptunium (Np). This has a half-life of 2⅓ days and decays by tossing out a beta particle (again a neutron becomes a proton). The number of protons has now increased to 94 and still another

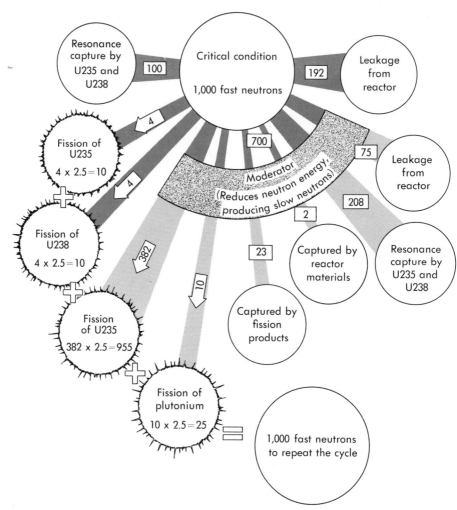

Figure 7-3. The neutron balance in a natural uranium reactor that is just critical. This sketch shows what might happen to 1000 representative neutrons out of the many millions present in a reactor. Note: Resonance capture means that a uranium nucleus captures a neutron without fissioning. (Courtesy of Westinghouse Electric Corporation)

element appears that does not exist in nature. It has been named plutonium (Pu). This decay process is written as follows:

$$_{92}U^{238} + {_0}n^1 \rightarrow {_{92}}U^{239} + \gamma$$
$$_{92}U^{239} \rightarrow {_{93}}Np^{239} + {_{-1}}e^0$$
$$_{93}Np^{239} \rightarrow {_{94}}Pu^{239} + {_{-1}}e^0$$

Plutonium, the granddaughter of U238, is a very important radioactive element with a long half-life of 24,000 years. After emitting two alpha particles and some gamma rays, it eventually decays to U235. Its importance lies in the fact that it is fissionable. It can be separated from uranium by chemical means and stored for future use. Some of the plutonium produced in a reactor is fissioned by slow neutrons even before it is extracted. (See Figure 7-3.) At present most of the existing plutonium in this country is reserved for military weapons, although some experiments are going on using plutonium as the fuel in reactors.

Release of energy and the production of heat

As a U235 nucleus fissions, it causes the sudden movement outward of the two fission fragments and two or three neutrons. Their combined kinetic energy totals about 200 Mev. In addition, as the fragments decay, they emit further radiation in the form of beta particles, positrons, and gamma rays. Now if you recall that billions of fissions occur in a second, you will readily see that a great deal of heat is produced. The heat results from the movement of the fragments and particles. We said earlier that in the fission of a nucleus there is a small loss of mass that is converted into energy. This energy takes the form of the kinetic energy of the moving fragments, which in turn is transformed into heat energy. This heat can be used for the purpose of power production, as you will read in the following chapter. In research reactors the heat is mainly a bother and has to be removed by a cooling agent.

HOW REACTORS ARE CONSTRUCTED

You already know that a reactor must have a core of fissionable material, a moderator to slow down neutrons, and control rods to control the chain reaction. In addition, there must be a shield to prevent the escape of dangerous neutrons and gamma rays, which would harm the people operating the reactor. There must also be a means of carrying off the intense heat produced by the reactor, a cooling agent. And there is, as well, a reflecting material used to bounce back neutrons that would otherwise leave the core and be lost in the shield. Usually, reactors start spontaneously once the

Figure 7-4. South face of the Brookhaven National Laboratory Reactor. Tons of pure uranium metal must be loaded through the holes in the shielding wall into the graphite moderator before uranium atoms can fission in a chain reaction. The holes can also be used to insert various substances to be irradiated by neutrons. (Brookhaven National Laboratory)

control rods are removed, because of stray neutrons knocked out by cosmic rays. Occasionally you might hear of a reactor that uses a neutron source. Figures 7-4 and 7-5 indicate some of the great variety that is found in the construction of reactors.

We shall now describe these various parts as they appear in the pool reactor at the Naval Research Laboratory (NRL) and also indicate how other reactors may vary in construction.

The *core* is, of course, the heart of the reactor. It is the part that contains the fuel, the name given to the fissionable material. In the first reactor, the fuel was natural uranium in solid form. This is still used today. However, more frequently, enriched uranium is used, either in solid or liquid form. *Enriched* means that there

Figure 7-5. Nuclear physicist checks the stainless steel core of a solution type reactor. The fuel consists of uranyl sulfate mixed with light water as the moderator. Heat is carried off by light water which circulates through the coils of stainless steel tubing. When in use, the core is surrounded by a graphite reflector and a heavy concrete shield. Fission is started by means of a plutonium-beryllium source and controlled by four boron carbide rods. (Courtesy of Atomics International)

is a greater than normal amount of U235. Since it is mainly the U235 that fissions, the greater the proportion of U235, the smaller the core needs to be to reach critical size. The reason is, of course, that with more U235, more neutrons will be produced. The NRL reactor core consists of enriched uranium in the solid form of plates made of a uranium-aluminum alloy. This core, being 90 per cent enriched, is only 21″ by 21″ by 24″. It is at the bottom of the vertical assembly that you can see in Figure 7-1.

To obtain pure U235 is a very difficult and expensive process because two isotopes of the same element have to be separated. Since they are chemically alike, chemical processes cannot be used. The most common method of separating U235 from U238 is to convert them to uranium hexafluoride (a gas) and then force the gas through a series of barriers containing thousands of tiny holes. The U235 hexafluoride, being slightly lighter, will rise more readily and can be collected and treated chemically to get the metallic U235. A new, more efficient method just perfected uses a centrifuge (like a cream separator in a dairy) to separate U235 from U238 in gaseous form.

There is one other fissionable material — U233. This is created from thorium and used in some power reactors. You will read about this in the next chapter. As we said before, experiments are being conducted in the use of plutonium as a fuel. The following chart indicates the fissionable materials and their sources. (The term *fertile* means that the material can produce a fissionable material by capturing neutrons.)

Source	Fertile	Fissionable
Uranium		U235 (in nature)
Uranium	U238 →	Pu 239
Thorium	Th 232 →	U233

As the chart shows, the only fissionable materials are uranium 235, plutonium 239, and uranium 233. Of these, uranium 235 is the only fissionable material found in nature, being one part in 140 of natural uranium. Plutonium 239 is obtained as a result of neutron capture by uranium 238, which is therefore called a fertile material. Uranium 233 is obtained as a result of neutron capture by thorium 232, which is also called a fertile material. A reactor must have a fissionable material. It may also have a fertile material.

Solid fuels are encased in an aluminum or stainless steel jacket (called cladding) to keep them from touching the cooling agent. The object is to prevent corrosion of the fuel and contamination of the cooling agent by radioactive atoms. In the NRL core the uranium is combined with aluminum in the form of an alloy.

Two types of reactors use the uranium in liquid form. In one, the uranium is combined with molten bismuth. Bismuth melts very easily and captures very few neutrons. In the other, a liquid compound of uranium is combined with heavy water.

The water in the NRL reactor serves as many as four purposes: moderator, shield, reflector, and cooling agent. Water makes an excellent moderator. As was said earlier, a particle is slowed down best by a particle of the same mass. Since water consists of so many hydrogen atoms, it is full of protons, which are about the same mass as neutrons, and therefore very effectively slows them down. Reactors with a core of natural uranium still use graphite as the moderator, as in the first reactor. Some use is also made of beryllium and of heavy water. Heavy water is superior to light water as a moderator because it absorbs fewer neutrons.

It is of vital importance to shield workers from the highly dangerous radiation — principally neutrons and gamma rays — produced in tremendous quantities during the operation of a reactor. The water in the NRL reactor serves this purpose. The neutrons are stopped by colliding with the hydrogen nuclei in the water, and the gamma rays lose their energy in repeated collisions with electrons. The collision of gamma rays and electrons produces the weird blue glow visible around the core, an effect known as Cerenkov radiation. As an additional shield, when the NRL core is at one end of the pool, it is backed by a barrier made of concrete, barium, and iron.

The graphite and the water in the NRL reactor act as reflecting agents to bounce neutrons back into the core, where they can be of use in causing fission.

Water is a common cooling agent or coolant. In the case of the NRL reactor, the core is suspended in the water. In the case of large cores that are mostly or entirely made of natural uranium, the water is circulated through the core by means of pipes. Other coolants that may circulate through pipes are gases (air, helium, carbon dioxide) and liquid metals (sodium, potassium, bismuth). Pumps keep the coolant circulating through the heat-producing core. The first reactor did not have a coolant.

In the NRL reactor the chain reaction is controlled by means of one stainless steel rod that reaches down into the core. In addition, there are three safety rods of boron-carbide that can be quickly dropped into the core if for some reason the reactor starts getting out of control, that is, if the rate of fission becomes too great. Some reactors have cadmium control rods, as did the first reactor.

No matter what materials are used, you can see that the purposes are the same: to produce neutrons, to maintain a chain reaction, to control it, to protect personnel, and to carry off the heat.

An essential part of any reactor is its detecting instruments. Those operating the reactor must know at all times how many fissions are taking place per second. If the rate increases beyond the desired point, then the control rod can be pushed in farther by remote control. The rate of fission is determined by the number of neutrons produced. The presence of neutrons is registered by a neutron detector, which is a kind of Geiger counter. The information is carried from the reactor to the control room. Outside the reactor, other instruments are used for the protection of personnel. These detect the presence of undesirable radiation outside the reactor and reveal leakage of radioactivity, if there is any.

WHAT ARE REACTORS USED FOR?

Before we can answer this question, we must realize that even in this new field of human endeavor the stage of specialization has been reached. Certain reactors have been built for specific purposes. Although in this chapter we are confining our discussion to research reactors, we must note in passing that certain reactors were built exclusively for the production of plutonium. Some were built to provide further knowledge as to how to build reactors. Some were built to study the possibility of large-scale power production. These have pointed the way to the nuclear power stations to be discussed in Chapter 8. Others, like the ones described in this chapter, were built to make use of the neutrons and gamma rays produced by the fission process. One reactor, at Oak Ridge, Tennessee, is devoted to the production of radioactive isotopes for sale to users. By 1963 there will probably be more than 200 reactors in the United States.

Use of gamma radiation

There are two main ways of using gamma rays. One way is to take a radioactive substance that emits gamma rays and permit the rays to strike the desired target. This use of gamma radiation is discussed in Chapter 10. The other way is to place an object in the path of the gamma rays that come directly from the core of a reactor. One purpose of reactors is to study the effect of gamma radiation on various materials. In the case of the NRL reactor, large objects can be lowered into the pool and irradiated. The NRL reactor produces as much gamma radiation as one ton of radium. The importance of this fact becomes clearer when we realize that only about three pounds of radium has ever been produced in the whole world, and only a tiny fraction of that is ever available for use in any one place.

Gamma rays from reactors are also used to study the effects of radiation on experimental animals. Knowledge gained in this way is applied to the treatment of radiation damage in human beings.

Use of neutrons

Aside from their principal function of producing fission, the most important uses of neutrons are for the production of radioactive isotopes and for research. A substance is made radioactive by being placed inside a reactor in such a position that neutrons can strike it and be captured. For example, cobalt 59 captures a neutron and becomes radioactive cobalt 60. In some cases irradiation by neu-

Figure 7-6. Production of radioisotopes. The material to be irradiated is in the little container that is being placed in the hole in the graphite tray. Once the tray is pushed into the reactor, it will be bombarded by neutrons. (U. S. Army Photograph)

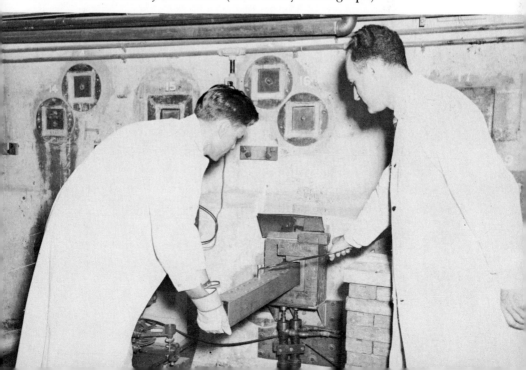

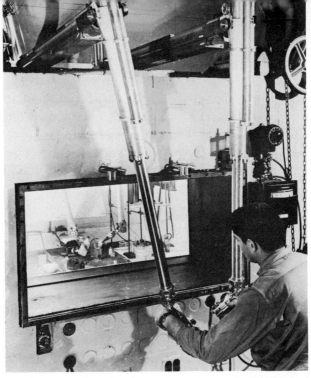

Figure 7-7. A scientist handles radioactive materials by means of "mechanical hands." He is separated from his work by a concrete barrier and a liquid-filled porthole. (Oak Ridge National Laboratory)

trons takes a few hours; in others it may take a few days or even longer.

There are various ways to get a material into a reactor for purposes of irradiation. In the case of a pool-type reactor, large objects can be lowered directly into the water of the pool. Smaller amounts of material can be inserted into the core of a reactor through a solid-type shield by means of openings left in the shield. The material to be irradiated is placed in compartments of long graphite trays, which are then inserted into the openings in the shield. (Figure 7-6.) When the correct time of exposure is up, the trays are pulled mechanically into a heavy lead box with walls about six inches thick. The box, mounted on a frame on wheels, is tested for radioactivity that might be escaping and then moved behind a lead and concrete wall. Human hands do not touch the isotopes. Mechanical arms remove them while the men who operate the arms watch through a specially shielded window. (Figure 7-7.)

The isotopes are purified and made into desired compounds by chemical processes, all done by remote control. The concentrated isotopes are then shipped in lead-lined containers, which are safe enough to be handled by ordinary railway express. Such packages are marked with the international radiation danger symbol. (See Figure 7-8.)

In the shield of the NRL reactor there is a graphite column with two openings into which material can be placed for irradiation by slow neutrons. It also has two small carriers called "rabbits," which can be sent by means of compressed air pressure through tubes to a spot near the core and then automatically removed.

We can get some idea of the tremendous quantities of neutrons involved in irradiation by neutrons from a figure that applies to the NRL reactor. In a certain area in the core, there are ten trillion (10^{13}) neutrons flowing each second per square centimeter. Clearly we must think in terms of trillions of neutrons.

Neutron irradiation is also used to change the physical properties of some materials. Fast neutrons can make certain metals harder and more resistant to wear. Slow neutrons can affect plastics, making them harder, stronger, and more resistant to tem-

Figure 7-8.   International radiation danger symbol.

CAUTION

RADIOACTIVE MATERIAL

perature changes. You probably know that most soft plastic containers in common use in the home cannot withstand boiling. But if they were irradiated in a reactor, they could. Plastic baby nursing bottles, which have been irradiated and can stand sterilizing heat, are now in production.

Neutrons for research purposes are usually used in the form of neutron beams, which are obtained by means of openings (called ports) in the reactor shield. The NRL reactor, for example, has six round beam ports, six inches in diameter, and one rectangular beam port, ten by twelve inches. They provide either fast or slow neutrons, depending upon their position in the shield.

With the aid of neutron beams, physicists can study the arrangement of atoms in materials. You may remember from Chapter 2 that the arrangement of atoms in materials can be studied by the patterns of the X-rays that are deflected by crystals.

But this method does not work so well in the case of atoms having very few electrons, since the X-rays are diffracted mainly by the electrons. In such cases neutrons are useful. For example, slow neutrons are scattered by the nuclei of hydrogen and thus reveal the position of the hydrogen atoms.

Fast neutrons, instead of being scattered by nuclei, have the power to knock atoms out of position and thus change their patterns. Then the change in the pattern is studied to see how it affects the properties of a material, such as its hardness or its ability to transmit heat or electricity.

Extra slow neutrons, called "cold" neutrons, are used to study the motion of atoms. The speed of the neutrons is affected when they are struck by moving atoms. Extra slow neutrons are obtained by letting slow neutrons pass through a special filter.

CHAPTER 8

NUCLEAR POWER

You know, of course, that "atomic energy" is the greatest potential source of power that man has yet discovered. He is just beginning to learn how to put it to use. The United States has begun to produce electricity from nuclear power and has a number of nuclear-powered submarines in operation and several nuclear-powered ships under construction. England, Canada, and Russia have also made progress in this field.

WHY USE NUCLEAR POWER?

The real importance of nuclear power to the world lies in the assurance that there will be ample nuclear fuels to meet any foreseeable requirements for electricity. Needless to say, the world's power needs are constantly increasing. It has been estimated that the power needs of the United States double every ten years or so. Although our supply of fossil fuels — coal, oil, and natural gas — is ample for years to come, it is not inexhaustible. Some day there will be little left. Sooner or later there will be a growing necessity to save dwindling supplies for purposes that cannot be filled by nuclear power — such as the use of coal for chemicals, dyes, and synthetics, and oil for small power-users such as cars and motorboats. Nuclear power is of special importance to countries that have always had a fuel shortage.

WHAT IS NUCLEAR POWER?

You are already familiar with the fact that during the fissioning process a tiny bit of mass is converted into energy. Let us now take a closer look at that fact and try to see just how much more energy is derived from nuclear fission than from the burning of fossil fuels. When a nucleus of U235 fissions, there is a loss of about $\frac{1}{5}$ of an atomic mass unit. In other words, the amount of mass that provides energy is the equivalent of one fifth of the mass of a proton or of a neutron. This amount of mass is about $\frac{1}{1175}$ of the entire U235 nucleus. The apparent loss of this very small portion of the nucleus results in the creation of about 200 Mev of energy, as explained in Chapter 6. How does this figure compare with the energy produced by the chemical reaction in the burning of fossil fuels? In such cases only the outer electrons are involved. The nuclei remain unaffected by the burning. The release of energy is only a few electron volts for each atom that reacts.

Weight for weight, the release of energy in the fission process is *two and one half million* times greater than in ordinary burning. It therefore takes 2½ million times more coal than U235 to produce the same amount of energy. Put another way, the fissioning of all the nuclei in a pound of U235 would produce as much energy as the total burning of 2½ million pounds of coal.

We know that nuclear energy appears as the kinetic energy of the fission fragments and of the emitted particles. The movement of these fragments and particles through the surrounding material creates heat. Since there are billions of fissions per second during the operation of a reactor, there is a tremendous amount of energy released. This energy can be used in two main ways: it can be permitted to run away with itself in the form of an explosion, or it can be controlled and used as heat for the production of power.

We shall first consider the second use.

NUCLEAR POWER PLANTS

Although to convert nuclear heat to power is a tremendously difficult engineering problem, it is very easy to understand the basic principle of this process. Conventional power plants burn fossil fuels to produce heat to produce steam to drive a steam turbine. A nuclear power plant "burns" nuclear fuels to produce the necessary heat. The reactor takes the place of the usual furnace.

The turbines then can turn the propellers of a ship or they can turn generators to produce electricity.

Nuclear power plants designed for the production of electricity consist of two main parts: one part is the reactor system; the other part consists of the steam turbines and generators. The basic problem is to transfer the heat from the reactor to the water that is to become steam. There are two principal methods of doing this. In one type of power plant, water is turned to steam right inside a "boiling water" reactor and then fed directly to the turbines. In the other type, the water is kept under pressure to keep it from boiling. This kind of reactor is called a "pressurized water" reactor. Inside a pressure chamber, water is heated by the fissioning core and then is pumped through the tubes of a heat-exchanger boiler. Here water surrounding the tubes is heated and changed into steam. The steam then flows to the turbines in an entirely separate set of pipes. The water in the two systems does not intermingle. The drawing in Figure 8-1 shows how the two water systems remain separated.

Figure 8-1. A diagram of the Shippingport, Pa., nuclear electric power plant. The heat generated in the pressurized water reactor is carried to four heat exchangers where it is converted into steam. (Drawing by Mildred Waltrip from *EXPLORING PHYSICS* by Brinckerhoff, Cross, and Lazarus, copyright 1952, © 1959 by Harcourt, Brace & World, Inc.)

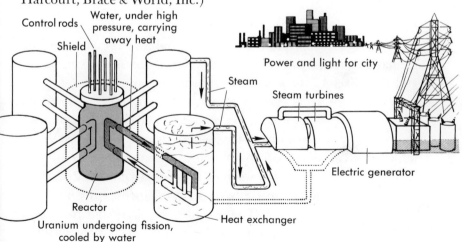

Control rods

Water, under high pressure, carrying away heat

Shield

Power and light for city

Steam

Steam turbines

Electric generator

Reactor

Uranium undergoing fission, cooled by water

Heat exchanger

Power reactor design is still in its infancy. The first production of electric power from a nuclear reactor was achieved on an experimental basis in 1951, when the Experimental Breeder Reactor at Idaho Falls, Idaho, produced 150 kilowatts of electricity. Since it has not yet been determined what combination of materials works best, many variations are being tried. The goal is to build a power plant that can some day produce electricity as cheaply as is done with conventional fuels. It is estimated that this goal can be reached by 1970. To give you an idea of the various approaches to the achievement of this goal, we will describe the world's first full-scale nuclear plant devoted to the generation of electricity for civilian use — the Shippingport Atomic Power Station at Shippingport, Pennsylvania — and then indicate briefly what other types of power plants are being developed.

SHIPPINGPORT ATOMIC POWER STATION

Sponsored by the Atomic Energy Commission and constructed by Westinghouse Electric Corporation, the Shippingport Atomic Power Station was put into operation in December of 1957. It produces 60,000 kilowatts of electricity constantly to serve the Pittsburgh area. Its heat source is a pressurized water reactor, the water being kept under a pressure of 2,000 pounds per square inch. The heat is transferred from the pressurized water in the primary system to the water of the secondary system by means of a heat exchanger. Water temperature averages 525° F. Four pipe loops pass through the pressure chamber containing the core and the primary water and carry the heated water out to the heat exchanger and then back to the reactor, as shown in Figure 8-1.

The reactor core consists of natural uranium (14 tons) and slightly enriched uranium (165 pounds). The natural uranium is in the form of uranium oxide pellets, which are placed inside hollow rods made of zirconium alloy. The enriched uranium is in the form of plates clad with an alloy of zirconium. Zirconium has been found to be especially resistant to corrosion by hot water and to radiation damage. The assembly of plates and rods forms a rough cylinder about six feet high and six feet in diameter. This assembly is placed inside the pressure vessel, which is a cylinder about thirty-one feet high and nine feet in diameter. Its walls are made of carbon-steel and are eight inches thick. The pressure vessel also contains the primary water, which enters at the bottom and leaves at the top.

Fission results mainly from slow neutrons, which are slowed down by the water, which functions as both coolant and moderator. There is also some fission by intermediate and fast neutrons. The U238 in the uranium oxide produces a certain amount of plutonium, slightly less than the amount of U238 that is used up. Since the creation of new fuel is *less* rather than *more* than the amount used up, this type of reactor is called a converter. Reactors that produce more fuel than they use up are called breeder reactors.

The rate of fission, and therefore the amount of heat produced, is regulated, as usual, by control rods. There are thirty-two of them, and they are made of hafnium, a metal that has been found to be a good neutron absorber. The rate of fission is automatically controlled by a temperature gauge that governs the mechanism that moves the rods. When the temperature of the water gets too low, the rods are adjusted to permit more fission. When the temperature of the water gets too high, the rods are moved farther in to slow down the fission rate.

The entire primary system is underground. It is housed in four containers made of steel one inch thick. Surrounding the containers is a five-foot thick concrete wall, which serves as a shield and as a building to contain the plant.

From this brief description of the Shippingport Power Station you may get the impression that a nuclear power plant is a rather simple thing. It most certainly is not. We have not gone into the many special engineering problems that arise from the ever-present radiation, such as the need for self-contained pumping mechanisms, the provision for repairing the reactor or for adding fuel to it, the provisions for removing radioactive elements that get into the primary water, the provisions for the removal of radioactive wastes, the provisions for safety in case of emergencies, and the various instruments used to measure a variety of things and to relay the information to various points.

So far we have mentioned only those types of power plants that use water as the heat conveyor (or coolant) and as the moderator. There are many other possible types of reactors that are now either being built or in the planning stage. One reactor using enriched uranium will have terphenyl as moderator and coolant. Terphenyl, a petroleum product related to benzine, is made entirely of carbon and hydrogen. It is less corrosive than water, does not need high pressure, and does not easily become radioactive. Another reactor will be moderated by graphite and cooled by liquid sodium. Sodium is an excellent heat transferer but tends to damage the pipes it flows through. Another reactor will be moderated by graphite and cooled by helium gas. Another will use heavy water as coolant and moderator. You can see how much variety is possible in the use of coolants and moderators.

Although the most common type of core is one of enriched uranium, other cores are also being used. One pressurized water reactor will have a core made of a mixture of enriched uranium and thorium. As the $U235$ fissions, some of the neutrons will be captured by the thorium, which will then decay to $U233$, a fissionable fuel. Since less fuel will be created than used up, this reactor is classified as a converter. It takes a few steps for thorium to become $U233$. Upon the capture of a neutron, thorium 232 becomes thorium 233. After $23\frac{1}{3}$ minutes it emits a beta paritcle (a neutron changes to a proton) and thus becomes protactinium 233. In 27.4 days the protactinium emits a beta particle and becomes $U233$. (Remember that these figures are half-lives and indicate in how much time half of the thorium present will go through a certain nuclear change). These changes are summarized as follows:

$$_{90}Th^{232} + {}_{0}n^{1} \rightarrow {}_{90}Th^{233}$$
$$_{90}Th^{233} \rightarrow {}_{91}Pa^{233} + {}_{-1}e^{0}$$
$$_{91}Pa^{233} \rightarrow {}_{92}U^{233} + {}_{-1}e^{0}$$

Other variations in the core are being tried out on an experimental basis. One core consists of a uranium compound in liquid form mixed with heavy water. Another uses liquid metal as a fuel. Uranium 233, dissolved in molten bismuth, flows through a graphite moderator. In one experiment, this kind of core is surrounded by a blanket of thorium, to breed U233. Experiments are also being made to determine whether plutonium can be used effectively as the fuel in a power reactor designed for the production of electricity.

A fast breeder is under construction. It is called fast because it has no moderator and therefore uses only fast neutrons. The fuel consists of an enriched uranium-molybdenum alloy clad with zirconium, with liquid sodium as the coolant. The U238 captures neutrons and produces plutonium. The breeding ratio is 1.2, meaning that 20 per cent more fuel is produced than is consumed.

NUCLEAR PROPULSION POWER

Nuclear power for propulsion is especially attractive because it eliminates the need for frequent refueling. Of course, this advantage is offset in part by the need for heavy shielding, which adds to the weight that must be carried around by the vehicle. The problem of weight is less serious in the case of water-borne vessels than in the case of aircraft. This fact partly accounts for the greater progress that has been made in the case of nuclear-powered submarines and ships than in the case of nuclear-powered aircraft.

By the end of 1960 the United States Navy had about fifteen nuclear-powered submarines, with twenty-two more under construction. The Navy is also building several nuclear-powered ships: an aircraft carrier, a guided-missile cruiser, and a guided-missile destroyer. The merchant ship *N.S. Savannah* (N.S. stands for Nuclear Ship) is expected to be in operation by 1961. Research continues on the development of nuclear-powered engines for rockets and planes.

The Nautilus

To illustrate the use of a nuclear reactor for propulsion, we will describe the *Nautilus* (Figure 8-2), the first nuclear-powered submarine.

In January of 1954 the United States Navy launched its first nuclear-powered submarine. The *Nautilus* is powered by a pressurized water reactor. The core, consisting of highly enriched uranium clad with zirconium, is suspended in the pressurized water. Fuel and water are enclosed in a carbon-steel chamber. As in the case of the Shippingport reactor, the primary water heated by the reactor transfers its heat to water in the secondary system by means of a heat exchanger. The steam is carried to the turbines, then to a condenser, where cool sea water converts the spent steam back into water, which flows back to the steam generator or heat exchanger to make more steam. The rate of power generation is controlled by hafnium rods.

The *Nautilus* has several major advantages over the ordinary type of submarine, the most important of which is its high sustained speed while submerged. While the older submarines could travel under water on battery at low speed for eight or even fifteen hours, they could run at top speed for only one hour, after which they would have to come near the surface to recharge their batteries with air-breathing diesel generators. The fuel core in the *Nautilus* provides enough power for at least two trips around the world (50,000 miles), much of which could be accomplished at high speed if that were desired. By running at high speed, a submarine is less subject to successful attack by depth charges, or even atomic weapons, because it is so difficult to find and track.

Although the reactor needs no air when submerged, the *Nautilus* must still replenish oxygen for breathing. This is done by carrying several tanks, which can be bled into the submarine living spaces when needed, and air purifiers that remove carbon dioxide. Another atomic submarine is known to have stayed submerged for sixty days.

The *Nautilus* makes better top speed submerged than a conventional type of submarine, 20 knots instead of 8.

The first *Nautilus* core lasted two years for a total of 62,562 miles, half of which distance she was submerged. It would take

Figure 8-2. Artist's conception of the nuclear-powered submarine S. S. Nautilus, launched on January 21, 1954. (U. S. Navy)

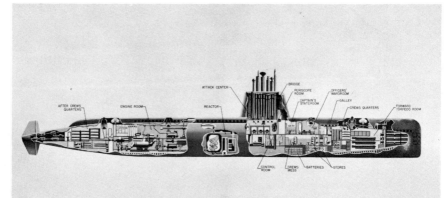

two million gallons of fuel oil to provide this much power.

When a reactor is refueled, the core is removed and replaced by a fresh unit. The old one is then sent to a processing plant where the remaining U235 and U238 are separated from the "ashes" or waste fission products created by the fission process. These "ashes" are then disposed of by being placed in containers that are buried deep in the ground or dropped into deep areas of the sea so that they will not be harmful to life. The salvaged uranium, after being processed, can be used again. The entire procedure must be carried out behind shielding by means of remote control apparatus.

Another atomic submarine, the *Seawolf,* used liquid sodium as the coolant and beryllium as the moderator. This reactor did not prove satisfactory and was replaced by the pressurized water type, which is the type now being used in the construction of all the atomic submarines.

In the spring of 1960 the *Triton* made an historic voyage, approximating Magellan's route around the world. It stayed submerged for eighty-four days and covered a distance of 36,000 miles.

ATOMIC HEATING PLANTS

Some buildings are heated by the circulation of hot water through radiators. Coal, oil, or natural gas is used to heat the water, and a circulating pump forces the hot water through the pipes and radiators. This type of heating system lends itself to the use of nuclear power, which would replace the usual furnace and boiler. Several large heating equipment companies are doing research on a small reactor that could serve this purpose. Naturally, such reactors would be very expensive at first. In addition, there would be the problem of providing enough uranium or thorium. In Greenland, a reactor under the ice supplies a research station with electric power and heat.

THE ATOMIC BOMB

So much has been written about the atomic bomb that we will not say much about it here, except to compare it with the kinds of reactors we have already described. In the case of a bomb, there is no question of controlling the chain reaction, of shielding the surrounding area from dangerous radiation, of slowing down the neutrons with a moderator, or of carrying off the heat by means of a coolant. The only thing is the core, which may be made of either U235 or Pu239. Fission is caused by fast neutrons. The core must be kept in two or more separate parts until the time of detonation. Otherwise the stray neutrons in the air would set off the chain reaction and cause the bomb to explode at the wrong time, though not with its full power. To create the desired explosion, it is necessary to bring the parts of the bomb together with great rapidity.

NUCLEAR EXPLOSIVES FOR PEACEFUL USES

Explosions can have their constructive uses, too. The government is investigating the possibility of using nuclear explosions for peaceful purposes. A study is under way in Alaska to determine whether it would be possible to excavate a harbor by this method.

Other uses for nuclear explosions are being studied. For example, it might be possible to get at oil deposits that are at present inaccessible because they are mixed in with rock, shale, or sand in a condition too thick for pumping. An underground nuclear explosion is expected to create enough heat to melt the oil and make it ready for pumping. Explosions might also be used to break up inaccessible mineral deposits.

Another idea being considered is the use of the heat from an underground nuclear explosion to produce power. It might also be possible to create radioisotopes by means of the released neutrons.

SUPERPOWER

So far in this chapter the source of power under consideration has been the fission process. But there is another type of nuclear reaction that may some day make fission seem old-fashioned. This is the type of nuclear reaction by which the sun creates its energy. It is called *fusion,* because the process involves the joining or fusing of atoms rather than their breaking up.

The sun, the greatest power plant known to us, converts its mass into energy at the rate of four million tons per second. The energy comes from the mass that is lost when four hydrogen atoms join to form one helium atom. In this process, which happens countless times per second, two protons are converted to neutrons.

One hydrogen atom has a mass of 1.008. Four hydrogen atoms have a mass of 4.032. A helium atom has a mass of 4.003. The mass apparently lost is .029 of one atomic mass unit. Since the energy equivalent of one atomic mass unit is 931 Mev, a single fusion of the four hydrogen atoms produces 26.999 or 27 Mev of energy. If four hydrogen atoms are merely burned in air, the energy produced is only about five electron volts. Although one fission of U235 produces about 200 Mev, we must remember that 235 mass units are involved, as compared with four in the case of fusion. Figuring the yield on a mass unit basis, fission produces $\frac{200}{235}$ or .85 Mev per mass unit, while fusion produces $\frac{27}{4}$ or 6.75 Mev per mass unit, or about eight times more energy than fission.

In order to cause nuclei to fuse, it is necessary to overcome their natural repelling action. The only way to make them come together and fuse is by using such great heat that the nuclei are forced to move back and forth with such speed (thousands of miles per second) that when they bump into one another, they fuse. The lighter nuclei are more likely to fuse than heavier ones because the heavier ones repel one another with greater force and would require even greater heat to be fused. Because fusion requires great heat, it is called a thermonuclear reaction. The only known source at present of the tremendous heat required (several hundred million degrees Centigrade) is that generated by the explosion of an atomic bomb, which, at this point, we had better call a fission bomb. Once a sufficient number of nuclei fuse, heat energy is released, the temperature rises, and there is enough heat to keep the fusion process going. If certain problems can be solved, man will be able to use the fusion process in a controlled way for power production. We will come back to this point a little later.

THE H-BOMB

You probably know that the H in H-bomb stands for hydrogen, because deuterium, or heavy hydrogen, is one of the elements that can be used in its manufacture. It is common knowledge that the United States and Russia have a stockpile of H-bombs and have tested a number of them. We all hope that the vast destructive power of these bombs will keep anyone from using them. The H-bomb is highly destructive, not only because fusion creates about eight times as much energy as fission, but also because in the case of the H-bomb there is no limitation set by the factor of critical size. In fission bombs, the core must be kept in separate parts, each of which is less than critical size. A quantity large enough to be of critical size will explode before the desired time. Thus there is a built-in limitation as to the size and power of fission bombs. In the case of the H-bomb, there is no such limitation. Actually, H-bombs have been tested that have been thousands of times more powerful than a fission bomb.

The actual materials curently used in our H-bombs are a military secret. However, we do know the basic principle involved. A quantity of material that will fuse (if heated to the necessary temperature) is combined with a fission bomb. As the fission bomb explodes, it generates enough heat to cause the fusion reaction to occur.

FUSING ATOMS

Before scientists can harness fusion power, they have the problem of creating it in a controlled fashion rather than in the form of an explosion. How are they going about achieving this goal? Although the actual achievement of sustained fusion is perhaps the most difficult problem scientists have ever been faced with, and although it may take fifty years before they solve it, it can be expressed in very simple terms: the problem is to make certain kinds of nuclei hot enough so that they will fuse.

There are several possible fusion reactions, which release varying amounts of energy. These reactions involve deuterons and tritons, nuclei with which you are already familiar. You will remember that the deuteron, the nucleus of deuterium — or heavy hydrogen ($_1H^2$) — consists of a proton and a neutron. Deuterium forms one part in 6,500 of ordinary water. A triton is the nucleus of tritium or extra-heavy hydrogen ($_1H^3$), which can be artificially produced in a number of ways. It consists of a proton and 2 neutrons. Supplies of tritium are being made in a government reactor by irradiating lithium with neutrons. This reaction is expressed thus:

$$_0n^1 + \,_3Li^6 \rightarrow \,_1H^3 + \,_2He^4$$

To distinguish more clearly between deuterons and tritons, it is convenient to use D and T instead of H for hydrogen. In their thermonuclear experiments, scientists regard the following reactions as most likely to produce fusion:

$$_1D^2 + \,_1D^2 \rightarrow \,_1T^3 + \,_1p^1$$
$$_1D^2 + \,_1D^2 \rightarrow \,_2He^3 + \,_0n^1$$
$$_1D^2 + \,_1T^3 \rightarrow \,_2He^4 + \,_0n^1$$

Now how are scientists trying to get these deuterons and tritons to fuse? To simplify the discussion, we shall speak only of deuterons.

First, deuterium in the form of a gas is introduced into a small vacuum chamber that has been exhausted until only about $\frac{1}{10,000}$ th of normal sea-level atmospheric pressure remains. This makes the deuterium gas very "thin," so that the deuterium atoms are comparatively far apart from one another in the vacuum chamber. Next, an electric current is applied to the thin deuterium gas. This ionizes the gas, separating the electrons from their nuclei, and also sets up a magnetic field. Now the gas is a good conductor of electricity, and the current that flows through is much stronger. The ions are heated by the current and move more rapidly. In this form of heated ions, the gas is known as a plasma, a term we shall use from now on. But even a strong current cannot, so far, make the plasma hot enough — and the goal may be as high as 350 million degrees Centigrade. So far, experiments have been carried out in which the plasma has momentarily reached a temperature of 33 million degrees Centigrade for $\frac{1}{1000}$ of a second.

Before we go any further, let us clear up the concept of this high temperature. A figure like 350 million degrees C. creates the impression that the plasma would be unimaginably hot in the usual sense of the word. In a sense this is true. The high temperatures do indicate very high speed or kinetic energy of the moving deuterons. However, we must remember that the plasma is not of normal density. The ions are quite far apart as compared with a normally dense gas. Now, if you can picture one single deuteron moving fast enough to reach a kinetic temperature of millions of degrees, you will realize that the total amount of heat it produces is very small. It has been estimated that a container of the kind of thin plasma we have been talking about, if heated to 350 million degrees Centigrade, would create enough total heat to warm up a cup of tea.

In order to attain higher kinetic temperatures (greater speed of the deuterons), scientists make use of the plasma's own magnetic field to squeeze the plasma into a smaller space. Another reason for the use of a magnetic field is to keep the ions from touching the walls of the container, for if they did, they would cool off and lose energy. The tendency for the plasma to expand and reach out to the walls of the vacuum chamber is greater in the case of denser gas. One reason for using a thin gas is so that the outward pressure of the heated plasma will be small enough to be held in by the magnetic field. Also, if the plasma were at normal density, it would create too much total heat, and the chamber walls would melt

Figure 8-3. The "pinch" effect in fusion experiments. The magnetic field compresses the plasma into a narrow channel in the center of the fusion chamber.

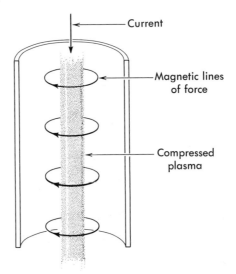

away. The plasma that envelops the sun is compressed together by the sun's tremendous gravitational force, but a substitute compressive force must be used on the small masses of plasma scientists work with.

FUSION EXPERIMENTS

Scientists are trying various methods and devices in an attempt to reach the high temperatures needed. The first device, created in 1952 by the Los Alamos Scientific Laboratories and interestingly named the Perhapsatron, employs what is known as the pinch effect (Figure 8-3). The plasma is in a cylindrical chamber and the electric current passing through creates a magnetic field that compresses or pinches the plasma into a narrow channel. (See also Figure 8-4.) A variation of the pinch tube is made in the form of a doughnut (Figure 8-5).

Figure 8-4. A linear fusion chamber. The discharge (white line) in the glass tube shows how the ionized gas (plasma) in the tube is "pinched" away from the walls of the tube, compressing the plasma. (Los Alamos Scientific Laboratory)

Figure 8-5. A doughnut-shaped fusion chamber. (Los Alamos Scientific Laboratory)

Another device, called a Stellarator, developed at Princeton's Forrestal Research Center, is an endless tube in the form of a figure 8 (Figure 8-6). The name comes from the hope that the temperatures reached will equal those of the stars. With this device scientists hope to create high temperatures by means of a rapidly changing magnetic field that will compress and expand the plasma several million times a second.

A third technique is that of the "magnetic mirror," being developed at the University of California's Radiation Laboratory. This was used to reach 33 million degrees Centigrade for $\frac{1}{1000}$ of a second.

A fourth technique, under investigation at Oak Ridge National Laboratory, is based on a different principle. Instead of starting with low-energy ions that are moving slowly, the plan is to give the ions high energies first and then trap them in a magnetic field where they will be forced to move at random and eventually collide and fuse. This method involves using an accelerator to speed up molecules of deuterium in the form of a beam and then to inject them across a magnetic field into a vacuum chamber.

WHAT HAPPENS IN A FUSION CHAMBER?

Now let us try to picture the events in a fusion chamber. Deuterons and electrons are in motion, controlled by the magnetic field. Deuterons are traveling about 1,500 miles per second. Their motion takes the form of a back-and-forth spiral, like the stripes on a barber's pole. Since the deuterons are comparatively far apart from one another in the thin plasma, it takes several seconds for them to collide and fuse. When a T^3 nucleus is formed, a proton is ejected. When an He^3 nucleus is formed, a neutron is ejected. The chances are 50-50. The protons remain in the plasma, trapped by the magnetic field. The uncharged neutrons escape to the outside. The presence of neutrons is one indication that fusion has occurred. So far, neutrons have been observed, but they have been caused by only a few fusions for periods of one millionth to one thousandth of a second.

The deuterons may also collide with electrons, but this is no help in the fusion process, as energy is lost to the outside in the form of X-rays. The sun also loses energy through radiation (or there would be no life on earth), but it has enough mass to spare this loss.

HARNESSING FUSION POWER

Once a sustained thermonuclear reaction is established, and scientists think it *can* be done even if the goal is many years in the future, there might be two principal ways of putting this energy

Figure 8-6. The Stellarator, a figure-eight-shaped fusion chamber. (Princeton University)

to work. One way would be to trap the escaping neutrons and use their kinetic energy to produce heat. This heat could then be used in the same way that heat from a fission reactor is used, to heat steam for the generation of electricity.

The other way would be to turn the energy of the fusion reaction directly into electrical energy without the intermediate step of heat energy. With this method, the outward pressure of the plasma itself against the magnetic field might be used to create current. In other words, the kinetic energy of the moving ions would be transformed into magnetic and then into electrical energy.

ADVANTAGES OF FUSION POWER

Although the problems are great and their solution far off, scientists in various parts of the world are seriously pursuing the possibility of creating fusion power because of what it would mean in terms of benefit to the world.

The most important advantage of fusion power over any other kind would be the unlimited supply of fuel. The prospect of getting fuel for power directly from the abundant waters of the earth is like a dream come true. Even though the amount of deuterium in one gallon of ordinary water is small — 1 part in 6,500 — it makes the gallon of water equal to about 300 gallons of gasoline as a fuel. Moreover, the cost of separating deuterium from water is about two or three cents per gallon of water processed.

In addition, fusion reactors would be safer than fission reactors. Fusion creates no radioactive fission fragments, since the nuclei do not break up as in the fission process. There would therefore be no problem of the disposal of radioactive wastes.

If the plasma tried to break through to the chamber walls, it would cool off and the fusion process would be interrupted. The only radioactivity to worry about would be that occurring in the structural materials as a result of neutron capture, but this is a relatively simple problem to handle.

CHAPTER 9

SMASHING ATOMS

Although people tend to speak of smashing atoms, it is important to remember that it is the nucleus of the atom that is being "smashed." The word "smash," though vivid and useful for conveying the idea that nuclei are struck with great force, is not entirely accurate, since it makes one think of something that is broken into many bits.

Now let us take a close look at "atom-smashing." When a bombarding particle enters the nucleus, it "excites" it. That is, it adds energy to the nucleus and disturbs the existing arrangement of particles. As a result, a new nucleus forms, and at the same time a particle is tossed out. Less often, a number of particles are ejected. Sometimes, however, the bombarding particle is captured by the nucleus without causing the emission of any particle. The nucleus becomes excited only to the point of sending out a gamma ray.

Although a great variety of results are obtained in "atom-smashing," nevertheless the nuclear changes must obey two fundamental laws: Conservation of Mass and Energy and Conservation of Charge. This means that after bombardment, the new nucleus and the newly tossed-out particle together will add up to the same amount of mass-energy and the same number of plus and minus charges as the original nucleus plus the bombarding particle. Every proton and every neutron can be accounted for.

Another pattern that can be observed is the relationship between the energy of the bullet and the energy of the new nucleus and the emitted particle. Now that so many disintegrations have been studied, physicists can pretty well predict what kind of new nucleus and emitted particle they will get if they use certain particles of known energies to strike certain targets. These studies are made by such means as cloud chambers, bubble chambers, scintillation counters, and nuclear emulsion film.

A third pattern concerns the way in which a radioactive isotope will decay. We will come back to that a little later.

The technical term for atom-smasher, the machine that "smashes" or disintegrates nuclei, is *particle accelerator*. This is a device to make charged particles go faster. Neutrons, having no charge, cannot be accelerated. The purpose of increasing the speed of positively charged particles is to give them sufficient energy to break through the repelling action of the nucleus that is being bombarded. As you know, like charges repel each other. Since the nucleus and the bombarding particle are both positively charged, they repel each other. The heavier the nucleus, the more positive charges (protons) it carries, and hence the greater the energy needed to penetrate it and to disintegrate the nucleus.

When electrons are accelerated, the case is somewhat different. Being negatively charged, they would not be repelled by the nucleus, but they do have to overcome the repelling force of the electrons. Before electrons can break up a nucleus, they must be accelerated to high energies. Even then, they do not have as strong an effect on nuclei as do positively charged particles.

Another purpose of accelerating electrons is to make them bounce off the nucleus. The way in which they bounce off and are scattered tells physicists something about the size and shape of the nucleus they strike. Another important use of accelerated electrons is the production of X-rays.

As you know, the first atomic bullets were alpha particles emitted by radium in the process of natural radioactivity. These have average energies of 6 Mev. Today, many accelerators produce particles having energies of hundreds of millions of electron volts. A few are in the billion class. The Cosmotron at Brookhaven National Laboratory on Long Island, New York, speeds up protons to energies of 3 Bev. The University of California's Bevatron at Berkeley produces 6-Bev protons. With their 10-Bev proton synchrotron, the Russians for a time had the most powerful accelerator in the world, until the end of 1959 when a 28-Bev proton-synchrotron was completed near Geneva, Switzerland, by the European Organization for Nuclear Research (CERN). Its member nations are Belgium, Denmark, France, West Germany, Italy, the Netherlands, Norway, Sweden, Switzerland, the United Kingdom, and Yugoslavia. In 1960, the United States completed what is now the world's largest accelerator, Brookhaven Laboratory's 30-Bev synchrotron. There are over 250 accelerators in the United States, slightly more than the number being used by a total of 27 other countries.

WHAT WE WANT TO KNOW ABOUT ACCELERATORS

You probably have a number of questions about accelerators in your mind right now. How are particles made to go faster and to attain greater energy? What kinds of particles can be accelerated? Where do they come from? What kinds of targets are used? What happens to the nuclei that are struck by the accelerated particles? What is atom-smashing good for? We hope that the information given in this chapter will give you at least partial answers to these questions.

A BIRD'S-EYE VIEW OF ACCELERATORS

If you look at the chart on page 138, you will get a quick, rough idea of what accelerators can do. First, you will note that there are several different types of accelerators. We will try to point out their basic differences. You can also see that they vary greatly in size and in the amount of energy they can impart. One of the most interesting points is the variety of particles used. In some cases the same accelerator is used for several kinds.

Accelerators can be divided into two main types. The direct current type (Van de Graaff generator and Cockcroft-Walton accelerator) uses high voltages to give the particles one strong push. All the others use low voltage but give the particle many small pushes as it goes along.

ACCELERATORS

Information given in this table was summarized from data given in a report by Gerald A. Behman, published by the University of California Radiation Laboratory in January 1958 and from a supplement published in January 1959 prepared for the Atomic Energy Commission. Information concerning the giant synchrotrons completed in 1959 and 1960 and the one scheduled for completion in 1961 was obtained directly from the Atomic Energy Commission.

Key to Symbols

e: electron   p: proton   d: deuteron   t: triton α: alpha particle

Type	U.S.	Other countries	Range of Size	Types of Particles	Range of energies in Mev
Cockcroft-Walton	23	52	2' to 16'	e,p,d,t,α, He^3 (rare: argon)	0.12 to 1 (rare: 4)
Van de Graaff	111	82	1.2' to 21'	e,p,d,t,α, He^3	0.3 to 8.5
Betatron	39	37	Radius of orbit 5" to 46"	electrons	3.5 to 100 (rare: 340)
Linear	32	28	Length of tube 1' to 260'	p,d,α nuclei of elements up to Ar^{40}	0.2 to 700
Cyclotron and synchro-cyclotron	36	39	Diameter of magnet pole pieces 6" to 184"	p,d,α nuclei of light elements	1 to 880
Electron synchrotron†	11	21	Radius of orbit 3" to 120'*	electrons	12 Mev to 6 Bev*
Proton synchro-tron†**	3	5	Radius of orbit 10.6' to 421'	protons	1 Bev to 30 Bev

† Smaller synchrotrons are two-pole type; larger ones are ring-type.

* Harvard-MIT, to be completed in 1961

** Includes those completed by 1960. See following chart.

THE WORLD'S LARGEST PROTON SYNCHROTRONS		
Location	Radius of Orbit	Maximum Energy in Bev
Brookhaven, Long Island	38'	3
Berkeley, California	50'	6.3
Dubna, U.S.S.R.	92'	10
Geneva, Switzerland (completed in November, 1959)	320'	28
Brookhaven, Long Island (completed in 1960)	421'	30

DIRECT CURRENT ACCELERATORS

In order to understand the principle of the direct current accelerator, you must remember that an electron volt is a measure of the amount of kinetic energy a particle has, as explained in Chapter 1.

Consider a particle that has one charge: an electron (one negative charge); a proton (one positive charge); a deuteron (one positive charge); or a triton (one positive charge). If one of these is given a push of a million volts, then the particle will have a kinetic energy of 1 Mev. In the case of an alpha particle, which has two positive charges (two protons), a push of a million volts will give the alpha particle a kinetic energy of 2 Mev. You can see from these examples that the energy of a particle will equal its charge multiplied by the voltage or amount of push that it receives.

The Cockcroft-Walton accelerator and the Van de Graaff generator were first built in the early 1930's, and improved models are still in use today. Both build up high voltages that are used to accelerate particles directly.

In the Cockcroft-Walton accelerator, particles are shot through a vacuum tube ranging in length from 2 to 16 feet. The particles move because they are repelled by a similar charge. Positively charged particles are obtained by passing a gas over an electric arc. In this way one or more outer electrons are stripped off and the gas is ionized. Thus, protons are obtained from hydrogen, deuterons from deuterium, tritons from tritium, and alpha particles from helium. Electrons are obtained from an electron gun like one in a TV tube. The particles are made to strike a target at the other end of the tube. The very high voltage is built up by means of a transformer-rectifier system. The Cockcroft-Walton accelerator has a top limit of 4 Mev, but usually the models operate at a particle energy below 1 Mev.

In the Van de Graaff generator, particles behave in the same way as in the Cockcroft-Walton, but the source of voltage is different. The Van de Graaff utilizes the principle of static electricity to obtain its voltage. In order to illustrate how it works, we will describe the 14-foot model at the Naval Research Laboratory in Washington, D.C. (Figure 9-1). This model is horizontal; some are vertical.

The photograph shows the shell to be transparent. This picture was taken with the steel shell off and then a picture of the shell was superimposed in a double exposure. A diagram of this model appears in Figure 9-2.

Charges are carried from the power supply to a comblike device that sprays them onto a moving, rubberized cotton belt operated by

Figure 9-1. A double-exposure photograph of the Van de Graaff accelerator at the Naval Research Laboratory showing the accelerating chamber inside the steel shell. (Naval Research Laboratory)

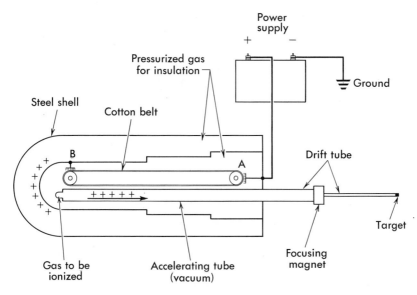

Figure 9-2. Diagram of Van de Graaff accelerator at the Naval Research Laboratory. Charges are sprayed onto belt at A and carried up to B.

a motor-driven pulley. At the other end of the belt, another comb-like device takes the charges from the belt and conducts them to the sphere-shaped end of the structure which encloses the tube and the belt. If protons are to be accelerated, a positive charge is used. If electrons are to be the bullets, a negative charge is used. The particles are then repelled down the accelerating tube, into the drift tube. They then pass through a magnetic field (focusing magnet), which can be adjusted so that particles of a predetermined energy are deflected along the desired path to the target.

Van de Graaff tubes vary in length from 1.2 feet to 21 feet and supply particles with energies ranging from 0.3 to 8.5 Mev. The Van de Graaff can be used for electrons, protons, deuterons, He³ nuclei, and alpha particles. The Tandem Van de Graaff, a new development, accelerates particles twice, once in each direction, thus giving them additional energy.

Direct current accelerators have their limitations. It is very difficult, because of insulation problems, to build up voltages greater than 8,000,000 volts. Other ways had to be found to accelerate particles so that the number of electron volts of energy finally acquired by a particle would greatly exceed the number of volts actually created by the machine. This problem was solved in a variety of ways by the construction of the linear accelerator, the betatron, the cyclotron, the synchro-cyclotron, and the synchrotron. All but one of these types of accelerators give particles many separate pushes, which add up to very high particle energies. In the case of the betatron, there is a single, continuous push, but the total energy results from an increasing magnetic field rather than from directly applied voltage.

LINEAR ACCELERATOR

The linear accelerator (Figures 9-3 and 9-4) consists of a series of tubes arranged in a straight line inside a vacuum cylinder. The charge on the tubes is constantly reversing at the correct moment in response to a series of radio oscillators. For example, let us assume we want to accelerate protons. Usually they are injected from a direct-current accelerator. The first tube will have a negative charge in order to pull the protons into the tube. As they enter, the charge is reversed to positive and repels them into the next tube, which is now negative to attract them. But it too changes to positive and sends the protons into the next tube, and so on until they strike the target. Each tube section is longer than

Figure 9-3.   Inside view of the linear accelerator at the Radiation Laboratory of the University of California, Berkeley. (University of California)

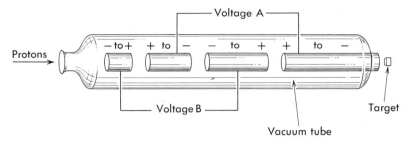

Figure 9-4. Diagram showing the principle of the linear accelerator. Voltage A is negative when voltage B is positive. When the particles approach the end of a tube, voltage B is negative and voltage A is positive.

the preceding one because the particles are traveling faster and faster. In the case of linear accelerators designed to use electrons, the tube sections are of the same length because electrons very rapidly reach maximum speed. Since all tube sections reverse charges simultaneously, particles that are moving faster need to go a greater distance so that they are at the end of a tube section when the charge reverses. Otherwise, they would not be propelled into the next section. In other words, slower particles in shorter tubes and faster particles in longer tubes take the *same* time to get to the end of a tube section.

The linear accelerator varies in size from 1 to 260 feet and produces energies from 0.2 to 700 Mev. It is used to accelerate mainly electrons, protons, and deuterons. It has the merit of being accurate, for it can aim the beam of particles with precision.

A proton linear accelerator under construction in England will be 891 feet long and is designed to produce protons of 1 Bev. The United States plans to build an electron linear aceclerator in California. It will be constructed underground and will extend for two miles. It is expected to produce electrons with energies of 40 Bev.

CIRCULAR ACCELERATORS
The remaining types of accelerators, which are circular in shape, make use of a magnetic field to direct the motion of the particles. Before we describe these, there is a simple experiment for you

to do that will demonstrate how a magnetic field influences the
path of particles. You will remember from Chapter 2 that moving

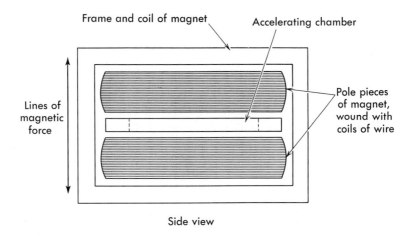

Side view

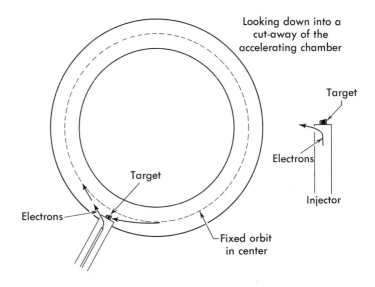

*Figure 9-5. Diagram showing the principle of the betatron. In
this model, the target forms part of the injector. The electrons in
orbiting must avoid striking the injector or the target until they
have reached the proper speed. This requires very exact timing.*

electrical charges are deflected by a magnetic field. If you did the experiment with your TV set, you saw how the ends of a bar magnet made the lines on the TV screen move. Now place a strong bar magnet flat against the TV screen while the set is on. Notice that between the magnetic poles the normally straight horizontal lines are now curved. The poles of the magnet are causing the electrons to move in a curved path.

THE BETATRON

As its name indicates, the betatron (Figure 9-5) is used to accelerate electrons. It is classified as an induction accelerator because it operates on the principle that a changing magnetic field can induce a current. (You can see how such a current is produced by doing the experiment that follows the description of the betatron.) A doughnut-shaped glass or porcelain vacuum tube is placed between the pole pieces of an electromagnet that are wound with coils of wire. Electrons are shot into the vacuum tube from an electron gun and are made to move in a fixed circular orbit in reponse to the force exerted by the magnet. The electrons move faster each time around because the magnetic field is constantly being increased. In less than a second they have traveled around the tube 100,000 times and have almost reached the velocity of light. The magnetic field then decreases and starts over again to produce the next burst of electrons. The target may be at the inner or outer circumference. In either case, the electrons are made to swing out of their orbit in the center of the tube to strike the target. The most common target materials are platinum and tungsten.

Betatrons in use today vary in size from an orbit radius of 5 inches to 46 inches and produce electrons ranging in energy from 3.5 to 340 Mev. The average is about 25 Mev, with several operating at 100 Mev. The principal use of the betatron is to produce high-energy X-rays. The highest energy betatrons can create X-rays that are more powerful than gamma rays from radium and that can go through a yard of steel. With such high-energy X-rays (about 100 Mev and over) it is possible to X-ray large blocks of metal or an entire Jeep. These X-rays might well be called gamma rays.

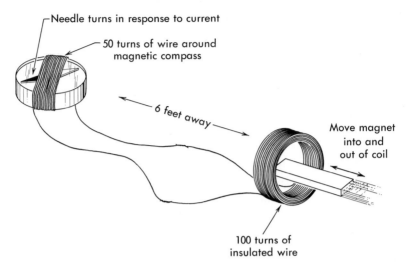

Needle turns in response to current

50 turns of wire around magnetic compass

6 feet away

Move magnet into and out of coil

100 turns of insulated wire

Figure 9-6. Induction experiment.

INDUCTION EXPERIMENT

You can easily observe how a magnetic field induces a current (Figure 9-6). You will need:

 a small pocket magnetic compass

 twenty feet of wire removed from the coil of an old electric
  bell *or* twenty feet of No. 24 magnet wire

 one hundred feet of insulated copper wire (any size)

 a magnet

 1. Wrap 50 turns of electric bell wire (or No. 24 magnet wire) around a small pocket magnetic compass.

 2. Make a coil of insulated copper wire by looping it 100 times, as shown. The opening in the coil should be large enough for the magnet to be slipped through.

 3. Join the two coils of wire by splicing them.

 4. Move the magnet into and out of the coil of wire. The compass needle will swing, showing the presence of a current in the wire surrounding the compass.

THE CYCLOTRON

The term "cyclotron" is a popular one and is often used to mean

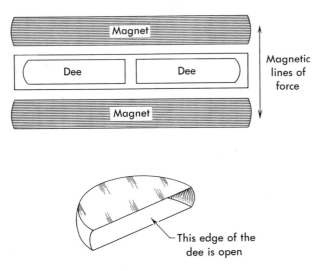

Magnet

Dee | Dee

Magnetic lines of force

This edge of the dee is open

Figure 9-7.   Diagram of cyclotron — side view.

"accelerator." However, technically, the term means a very specific type of accelerator. The cyclotron was the first circular accelerator to be used for positive ions. It accelerates protons, deuterons, alpha particles, and nuclei of light elements (up to nitrogen, No. 14).

A flat, round metal box is mounted horizontally between the poles of a large electromagnet so that the lines of force are perpendicular to the plane of the box (Figure 9-7). Inside the box there are two copper semicircular hollow boxes called dees because they are shaped like a capital D. They look like two halves of a giant pillbox.

The dees are connected to a powerful electrical supply that gives off an alternating current that changes millions of times a second. (Ordinary alternating current reverses 60 times a second.) The ion source is in the center between the dees. Particles are pushed in ever-widening circular orbits, moving faster each time around (Figure 9-8). Their faster speed and wider orbits combine to make each revolution take the same amount of time. The strength of the magnetic field and the frequency of the voltage applied remain constant. (Frequency is the number of times per second that the voltage is reversed.)

Let us follow a single proton in its trip around (Figure 9-9).

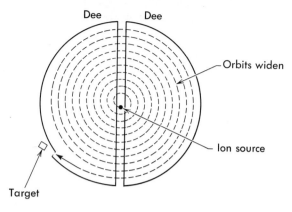

Figure 9-8. In the cyclotron, particles move in ever-widening circular orbits.

Imagine that Dee No. 1 is negatively charged for a tiny fraction of a second. It therefore attracts the proton. The magnetic field keeps the proton moving in a circular path. When the proton reaches the gap, Dee No. 1 becomes positive and Dee No. 2 becomes negative. The proton is therefore repelled by Dee No. 1 and attracted by Dee No. 2.

Since there are two gaps in each revolution, the proton receives two pushes each time around. Each time it moves faster and in a larger orbit. When its orbit is nearly as large as the chamber itself, it is pulled out of orbit by a highly charged negative plate and allowed to strike the target.

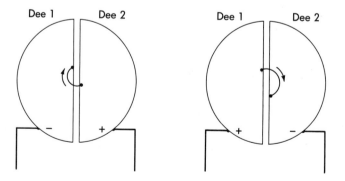

Figure 9-9. In the cyclotron, alternating voltage pushes the particles from one dee to the other.

The advantage of the cyclotron over a direct-current accelerator is shown in the following figures. The Van de Graaff takes 8 million volts to produce protons with a kinetic energy of 8 Mev. A cyclotron can produce protons of 8 Mev by using as little as 50,000 volts.

The cyclotron cannot accelerate protons beyond approximately 20 Mev. At this point the protons begin to increase in mass. This effect, of having particles increase in weight as they gain more energy, is known as the *relativistic effect* because it is caused by factors which are explained by the theory of relativity. In the case of large objects moving at what we call high speeds, such as jet planes, the increase in weight is too slight to be of any importance because these speeds are really low in comparison with the speed of accelerated particles. But in the case of particles the difference becomes very marked, particularly as the particles approach the speed of light. For example, a proton accelerated to 938 Mev weighs twice as much as a proton at rest.

In a cyclotron, protons that have begun to increase in mass no longer gain enough additional speed to make up for the fact that they are traveling in ever-widening orbits. Thus, they do not reach the gap between the dees in time to receive the usual push from the alternating voltage. To solve the problem of accelerating protons beyond speeds at which the relativistic effect occurs, scientists created a variation of the cyclotron known as the synchro-cyclotron. This has only one dee. Protons travel in ever-widening circular orbits, receiving their pushes from alternating voltage which is applied at the points where they enter and leave the dee, which is open at its straight edge. The frequency of the voltage changes to keep step with the protons, insuring that they will arrive at the proper moment to receive their electrical push.

The diameters of the magnets in the various cyclotrons and synchro-cyclotrons range from 6 inches to 184 inches. Energies range from 1 Mev to about 880 Mev, with the synchro-cyclotrons reaching very much higher energies than the cyclotrons, for the reasons just given.

THE SYNCHROTRON

As synchro-cyclotrons became larger and larger, they reached a point at which it became too expensive to construct them because of the huge quantities of iron needed for their magnets. To meet this problem, a new design was created, that of the synchrotron, which is doughnut-shaped and consequently uses much less iron for its magnets. Its name comes from the fact that an increasing magnetic field is accompanied by the increased frequency of the alternating voltage. In other words, the magnetic field and the electrical field are kept in step with one another or synchronized.

There are two distinct types of synchrotrons, one for electrons and one for protons. The same machine cannot be used for both. For one thing, electrons reach their maximum speed much faster than protons, and so the same timing mechanism could not be used for both. For another, protons, being so much heavier, are much harder to bend in a magnetic field and require the use of much bigger machines.

Figure 9-10. The Cosmotron at Brookhaven National Laboratory. The Van de Graaff generator shown in the foreground injects protons into the Cosmotron, which then accelerates them to energies of 3 BEV. (Associated Universities, Inc.)

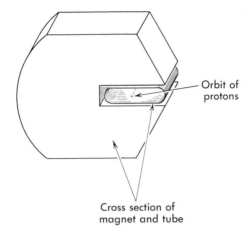

Orbit of protons

Cross section of magnet and tube

Figure 9-11. Diagram of the cross section of the magnet and accelerating tube in the Cosmotron.

Electron synchrotrons were developed first and range in size from those having an orbit radius of 3 inches to those with an orbit radius of 120 feet. (The larger orbit is in the ring-type magnet arrangement.) The energies of the electrons range from about 12 Mev to 6 Bev, this top figure representing the Harvard-MIT accelerator scheduled for completion at Cambridge in 1961.

Proton synchrotrons are the giants of the accelerator field, at least at present, their orbit radii ranging from 10.6 feet to 421 feet, their energies from 1 Bev to 30 Bev.

Brookhaven's Cosmotron
The Cosmotron was the first proton-synchrotron built in the United States. Its name is derived from the fact that it reaches the energies of some cosmic rays.

In the Cosmotron (Figure 9-10) there are 288 C-shaped magnets wound with copper wire and supplied with direct current. The magnets are 8 feet high and are massed in four sections. In the space between the poles of the magnets (Figure 9-11), a vacuum chamber about 6 inches high and 36 inches wide forms a circle about 75 feet in diameter. Particles travel within it in a fixed circle, except for four straight sections of the chamber, which measure 11 feet each.

As Figure 9-10 shows, a Van de Graaff generator is used to inject high-speed protons into the vacuum chamber. At a certain point in one of the straight sections, acceleration of the protons takes place by means of a cavity excited by a high-power radio frequency amplifier. (There is a rapid alternation between positive and negative charges.) Within one or two seconds, the protons are traveling 178,000 miles per second, close to the speed of light, have made 3,000,000 trips around, and have reached their maximum energy of 3 Bev.

Berkeley's Bevatron
The Bevatron at the University of California in Berkeley, California, derives its name from the fact that it gives particles energies of billions of electron volts. Protons, injected from a linear accelerator, reach energies of 6.3 Bev. The Bevatron resembles the Cosmotron, with four sections of magnets joined by straight-line sections. It is larger than the Cosmotron, being 100 feet in diameter.

Brookhaven's alternating gradient synchrotron
The capacity of this giant synchrotron to give protons energies of 30 Bev depends upon two main factors: the arrangement of the magnetic field and the large radius of the orbit around which the particles travel. The doughnut is 842 feet in diameter and about half a mile in circumference. One advance over preceding designs is the fact that the particles are focused into a narrow beam instead of wandering off to the sides of the acceleration chamber. With this intense and powerful beam, physicists now have the means of unlocking more of the secrets of the nucleus.

DIFFERENT KINDS OF BULLETS
You already know that the atomic bullets used in accelerators are electrons, protons, deuterons, tritons, alpha particles, and a few light nuclei. In addition, neutrons are used for bombarding nuclei. But they can be obtained only as the result of bombardment, as

they are emitted by excited nuclei. Therefore, one of the charged particles must be used to disintegrate a nucleus, which, in turn, emits a neutron. For example, deuterons aimed at heavy ice (ice made from heavy water, which contains $_1H^2$) yield an abundance of neutrons.

$$_1H^2 + {}_1H^2 \rightarrow {}_2He^3 + {}_0n^1$$

High energy gamma rays also cause disintegration, as do sufficiently high-energy X-rays.

Every element can be disintegrated. However, it is more useful to work with certain elements than with others. Targets are most commonly in the form of a solid, less often a gas, and rarely a liquid.

WHAT IS EMITTED BY THE TARGET?

Because the types of particles emitted vary with the energies of the bullet and the kind of nucleus disintegrated, a great variety of reactions have been observed. The following chart shows some of these.

The first letter indicates the bullet, the second the emitted particle.

α, p	p, α	d, α	n, α	γ, n
α, n	p, n	d, p	n, p	γ, α
α, γ	p, γ	d, n	n, 2n	γ, p
α, np	p, d	d, 2n	n, γ	e, p
	p, α, γ		n, d	e, n

α — alpha	d — deuteron	γ — gamma
p — proton	n — neutron	e — electron

Fission of several elements lighter than uranium has been achieved by bombardment with alpha particles and deuterons. However, fission is normally associated with the operation of a reactor.

MAN-MADE ISOTOPES PRODUCED BY BOMBARDMENT

Let us turn our attention now to the new nucleus that results from the bombardment. But let us not forget that new nuclei are also created during the operation of a nuclear reactor. Whatever is said here about the isotopes produced by bombardment in an accelerator applies equally well to the reactor-created isotopes.

Although some of the new nuclei are stable, we are concerned here mainly with what happens to the unstable or radioactive ones. These may be isotopes of the target element or of another element. Like all radioactive nuclei in nature, the artificially created ones try to return to a stable state by emitting radiation. Certain patterns may be observed, depending upon whether the unstable nucleus has too few or too many neutrons. If a nucleus has too few neutrons, it can reach a stable condition in most cases by emitting a positron or, less often, by capturing an electron from the nearest orbit. If it has too many neutrons, it will emit a beta particle. Let us see what happens in each of these instances.

Stable phosphorus is $_{15}P^{31}$, with 15 protons and 16 neutrons. One radioactive isotope is $_{15}P^{30}$ with only 15 neutrons. This isotope emits a positron $(_{+1}e^0)$ and becomes silicon, one step lower in the Periodic Table.

$$\text{Equation:} \quad {}_{15}P^{30} \rightarrow {}_{14}S^{30} + {}_{+1}e^0$$

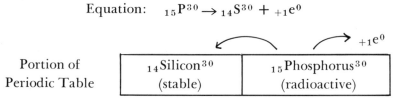

Portion of Periodic Table	$_{14}$Silicon^{30} (stable)	$_{15}$Phosphorus^{30} (radioactive)

There is no change in mass, but since a positive charge has been lost, a proton has been replaced by a neutron.

Capturing an electron (which is negative) works the same way as losing a positron (which is positive). The net effect is the same. Let us see how electron capture takes place. Stable beryllium is $_4Be^9$ with 4 protons and 5 neutrons. Radioactive $_4Be^7$ has only 3 neutrons. The nucleus captures an electron from the K shell as shown in Figure 9-12.

This process is known as K-capture. Another term is "orbital electron capture." The captured electron combines with a proton to make a neutron. Now there are 4 neutrons and 3 protons. The new element is lithium, which has 3 protons. The missing electron

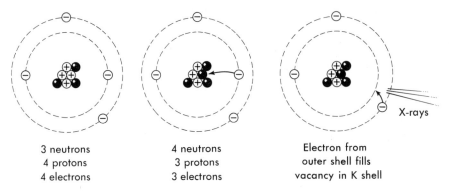

3 neutrons	4 neutrons	Electron from
4 protons	3 protons	outer shell fills
4 electrons	3 electrons	vacancy in K shell

Figure 9-12. Electron capture by a beryllium nucleus. Electron from outer shell fills vacancy in K shell.

in the K-shell is replaced by one from the outer shell and X-rays are produced. In this case, too, there is no change in mass. But a proton has been replaced by a neutron.

$$\text{Equation:} \quad {}_4\text{Be}^7 + {}_{-1}\text{e}^0 \rightarrow {}_3\text{Li}^7$$

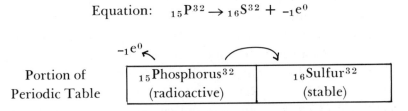

Portion of Periodic Table	${}_3$Lithium^7 (stable)	${}_4$Beryllium^7 (radioactive)

Now we come to the opposite situation, in which a nucleus has too many neutrons. Let us consider another radioactive isotope of phosphorus — ${}_{15}\text{P}^{32}$. This has 17 neutrons. It emits a beta particle (${}_{-1}\text{e}^0$) and becomes an isotope of sulphur, one step *higher* in the Periodic Table.

$$\text{Equation:} \quad {}_{15}\text{P}^{32} \rightarrow {}_{16}\text{S}^{32} + {}_{-1}\text{e}^0$$

Portion of Periodic Table	${}_{15}$Phosphorus^{32} (radioactive)	${}_{16}$Sulfur^{32} (stable)

Again there is no change in mass. But a neutron has been replaced by a proton.

Any one of these three types of decay may be accompanied by the emission of gamma rays.

Some radioactive isotopes take more than one step to reach stability. The result of the first step is known as the daughter element. The next is the granddaughter, and so on.

CREATING MATTER FROM ENERGY

With sufficiently high energies it is possible actually to create particles that weren't there before. For this purpose bombarding particles of very high energies are needed. With such particles physicists have created in accelerators practically all known particles, including those that are produced by cosmic rays, such as mesons and hyperons. (See Chapter 4.) For a complete table of subatomic particles (subatomic meaning smaller than the atom itself) see Appendix B.

For example, mesons, first produced by the Cosmotron, can be produced by bombardment in a variety of ways. The following chart shows only some of the ways. Different results are obtained from the same combinations of particles because of differences in their energies. The symbol pi (π) represents one type of meson, the pi meson, also known as a pion, which occurs in three forms: with a positive charge, with a negative charge, and with no charge.

$$\gamma - \text{gamma ray} \qquad \text{n} - \text{neutron} \qquad \text{p} - \text{proton}$$

$$\gamma + \text{p} \rightarrow \text{n} + \pi^+ \qquad \text{p} + \text{p} \rightarrow \text{p} + \text{n} + \pi^+$$
$$\gamma + \text{p} \rightarrow \text{p} + \pi^0 \qquad \text{p} + \text{p} \rightarrow \text{p} + \text{p} + \pi^0$$
$$\gamma + \text{n} \rightarrow \text{p} + \pi^- \qquad \text{p} + \text{n} \rightarrow \text{p} + \text{p} + \pi^-$$
$$\gamma + \text{n} \rightarrow \text{n} + \pi^0$$

Notice in these equations that the sum of positive and negative charges on one side of each equation equals the sum of the charges on the other side. This is another illustration of the law of Conservation of Charge. Notice also that there is more mass in the right-hand side of each equation. This does not violate the law of Conservation of Mass. Remember that the additional mass was created out of energy, and mass and energy are interchangeable.

Because accelerators can now produce particles that used to be observed only in cosmic ray collisions, cosmic ray study is now carried on in laboratories as well as by means of detecting instruments sent to high altitudes. For example, disintegrations created by the Bevatron can be filmed by the method of nuclear emulsion stacks, which are then mailed for microscopic examination to physicists working in laboratories that do not possess such an effective accelerator.

NEW PARTICLES

Bombardment by high-energy particles has resulted in the discovery of new particles hitherto unknown. In 1955 the antiproton was discovered by means of the Bevatron. Later, the antineutron was also discovered at Berkeley. These two particles are examples of what is known as antimatter. Although we have not used this term until now, you have already met a particle that consists of antimatter — the positron, which has the same mass as the electron but with a positive instead of a negative charge. When a positron encounters an electron, both particles are annihilated, releasing all of the mass as energy.

Similarly, any of the other particles can be annihilated by encountering their antimatter partners. Now normally the particles that make up the matter of our world do *not* meet their opposites. If they did, they would disappear. A world cannot exist with both types of matter. But, since antimatter can appear momentarily in our world, physicists speculate about the possible existence, outside our own galaxy, of worlds made entirely of antimatter. In such a world a hydrogen atom would have an antiproton as a nucleus with a positron in orbit. An antiproton has the same mass as a proton but a negative charge.

Evidence for the existence of antimatter, suggested by the behavior of the positron, came with the creation of matter from energy in accelerators. Physicists discovered that protons and antiprotons were created in pairs. Think of a beam of 6 Bev protons from the Bevatron striking a target and causing nuclei to disintegrate into a variety of particles. These particles are piped into a hydrogen bubble chamber where their various tracks are photographed and analyzed. Since 6 Bev is much more energy than is needed to break up a nucleus, there is an excess of energy present, which is converted into matter. When a proton-antiproton pair has been created out of this excess energy, the antiproton, upon being piped into the hydrogen bubble chamber, will, if it encounters a hydrogen nucleus (proton), cause its annihilation as well as its own. The energy represented by the proton and antiproton that have disappeared then takes the form of several mesons of a certain mass, traveling at certain speeds. It is the presence in the bubble chamber of these mesons that tells the physicist that a proton and an antiproton have annihilated each other. Only this particular nuclear event is capable of producing these particular mesons moving at these speeds.

At the time the positron was identified by Anderson in 1932 during his observation of cosmic rays, the existence of an antiproton was suspected, but it took almost twenty-five years before it was actually observed in 1955. It could not have been created in the laboratory before the existence of the Bevatron. The only other source of energy capable of creating antiprotons is cosmic radiation. So far, it has not been definitely established that antiprotons have been observed in cosmic ray collisions.

The antineutron was discovered as a result of the creation of the proton-antiproton pair. Under certain circumstances, when the proton and the antiproton come close to each other but not close enough to annihilate each other, an electrical charge is transferred from one to the other, making them both electrically neutral. The proton becomes a neutron and the antiproton becomes an antineutron.

In 1959 the antilambda hyperon was created. An antiproton from the Bevatron struck a proton in Berkeley's new liquid hydrogen bubble chamber and produced a lambda and an antilambda hyperon. These particles, having no charge, were not observed directly but were identified by their charged decay products. (See Appendix B for a complete list of particles.)

NEW ELEMENTS
Particle bombardment has also created new elements that do not exist in nature.

93 Neptunium (Np)	96 Curium (Cm)
94 Plutonium (Pu)	97 Berkelium (Bk)
95 Americium (Am)	98 Californium (Cf)

99 Einsteinium (Es)   101 Mendelevium (Md)
100 Fermium (Fm)   102 Nobelium (No)

The new elements are called transuranic elements because they are beyond uranium in the Periodic Table. In order to produce these elements, it is necessary to bombard a naturally occurring heavy element first. Then the new element produced can be used as a target to make an element of a higher atomic number. In the creation of the new elements so far produced, uranium has been used as the initial target. A number of different isotopes have been produced for each element. Some isotopes are made in accelerators, others in a reactor. Some can be made both ways. To give you some idea of the variety of ways in which these new isotopes can be produced, we will use three of the seven isotopes of fermium as an example.

A nucleus of U238 can become a nucleus of Fm 250 by being bombarded with a nucleus of ordinary oxygen. In the process, four neutrons are ejected.

$$_{92}U^{238} + {}_8O^{16} \rightarrow {}_{100}Fm^{250} + 4n$$

To make Fm 252, Cf 250 is bombarded with the nucleus of ordinary beryllium. In the process, an alpha particle and three neutrons are ejected.

$$_{98}Cf^{250} + {}_4Be^9 \rightarrow {}_{100}Fm^{252} + {}_2He^4 + 3n$$

Nuclei of U238 can become nuclei of Fm 254 in a reactor by capturing enough neutrons.

$$_{92}U^{238} + \text{multiple neutron capture} \rightarrow {}_{100}Fm^{254}$$

In this last case, some of the neutrons change to protons during the process.

WHAT ARE ACCELERATORS GOOD FOR?
The prinicipal use of accelerators is for nuclear research. They are often called the microscopes of nuclear physics. They provide the only means of "seeing" inside the atom (Figure 9-13). By bom-

barding various nuclei with high-energy particles, physicists are attempting to understand the structure of the nucleus. What holds the nucleus together? Why are there so many short-lived particles? Why do certain particles exist at all? Are there any more to be discovered? As higher and higher energies are reached in the new accelerators being constructed and envisioned, doubtless more knowledge will be gained about the basic nature of matter.

Some practical, applied uses have been found for accelerators. Although it is easier and less expensive to create radioisotopes by means of irradiation in a reactor, accelerators are used extensively to make radioisotopes that cannot be prepared or obtained in a concentrated form by other methods. Bombardment of certain targets results in the production of X-rays and gamma rays, which

Figure 9-13. This photograph is an enlargement of the tracks made by particles in nuclear emulsion film. The incoming particle presumably was a neutron and therefore is invisible. The neutron hit the nucleus of an atom of the emulsion, exploding it into 17 different visible particles, which flew out forming tracks in a star-shaped pattern. In general, the heavy lines are made by slow particles, protons, and the light lines by lighter, faster particles. The black spots are grains in the emulsion. The tracks are 50 times actual size. The Cosmotron at Brookhaven National Laboratory produced the accelerated particles, which, in striking the target, caused the emission of the neutron that hit the nucleus in the emulsion. (Brookhaven National Laboratory)

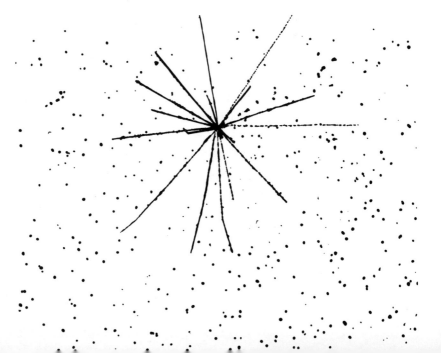

are used for taking pictures of thick objects and for treating cancer. Particle beams are also used for the sterilization of packaged drugs, surgical dressings, and even food.

The proton beam produced by the Bevatron has been used in place of the surgeon's scalpel. Sometimes, when an overactive pituitary gland produces too many hormones, which activate breast cancer, it is desirable to destroy the gland in order to control the cancer. The proton beam is used to destroy the gland. In this bloodless form of surgery, the beam is directed sharply on the target from many different angles. Thus the atomic surgeon is able to destroy a tiny area of tissue without harming the surrounding area to any large degree. The patient remains conscious and feels no pain. The physician directs the operation from a shielded room by means of television. It would be dangerous for him to remain in the treatment room because of the scattering of the proton beam.

Accelerators are being used to enlarge our knowledge of biology. By directing beams of X-rays and of various charged particles at living tissue of experimental animals and at plant tissue, scientists study the effects of radiation. For example, electron beams are directed at the skin of anesthetized rats and their effect analyzed. Neutron beams also are used in radiation studies. They are obtained by directing deuterons at a target of deuterium: $_1H^2 + _1H^2 \rightarrow _2He^3 + _0n^1$. The target nuclei become nuclei of helium, and the emerging beam of neutrons is directed at the tissue to be irradiated. It has been discovered that neutrons damage cells by interacting with the nuclei of their atoms.

EXPERIMENT: VAN DE GRAAFF GENERATOR

You can make a simple, safe Van de Graaff generator at home from easily obtained parts (Figure 9-14). With it you will be able to generate enough voltage to create a high-voltage spark. Although you will not be able to smash atoms with this generator, you can learn how a real Van de Graaff works. It is best to use this generator on a dry day or in a steam-heated room. Too much moisture in the air causes leakage of the static electricity and therefore will make the experiment less rewarding.

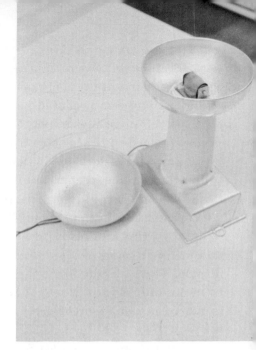

A   B

Figure 9-14.   Homemade model of the Van de Graaff generator. As the motor-driven pulley turns, friction of the wire screen (or lamb's wool, as in Figure 9-14g) against the rubber belt at the bottom of the generator (View a) causes electric charges to be picked up by the belt, which then carries them up to the top of the generator (View b), where they are picked off by the wire screen and discharged into the space formed by the two pans (View c). After a few minutes of operation, enough charges collect to create visible sparks.

You will need

- a rectangular aluminum baking pan, 3 to 4" deep
- two muffin-warming pans or two circular aluminum baking pans, 3 to 4" deep
- a tall plastic juice container that has a rim
- two sections of broomstick each 2" long to be used as pulleys
- a hand drill with wood and metal bits
- rubber cement, glue, and vaseline or oil
- 18 $\%_{32}$" machine screws or $\frac{1}{8}$" stove bolts, $\frac{3}{4}$", with nuts
- two headless nails, 3" long
- metal shears

C

√ two small angle irons
√ a piece of lamb's wool, attached to the hide, 2″ by 2″
two pieces of rubber or plastic tubing, about 1″ long
√ a strip of thin sheet rubber, 1½″ wide and twice the height of the juice container. Bicycle inner tube may be used.
√ two pieces of aluminum foil large enough to wrap around the cylindrical surfaces of the broomstick pieces
a toy motor of the type sold in hobby shops that runs on one or two dry cells
a piece of copper or aluminum window screening 2″ by 2″
three thin strips of wood about 1″ by 4″ (exact size depends upon the size of the container opening and the position of screws used to attach the motor; see Figure 9-14h.)
5 feet of insulated copper wire

How to assemble the generator

1. Cut the bottom off the plastic juice container. With the rectangular baking pan upside down, place the rimmed opening of the container in the center of the pan and draw its circular out-

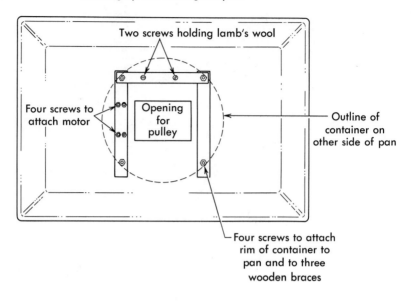

View of screws and braces
(Looking up into rectangular pan)

Two screws holding lamb's wool

Four screws to attach motor

Opening for pulley

Outline of container on other side of pan

Four screws to attach rim of container to pan and to three wooden braces

Figure 9-14d.   Subassembly A.

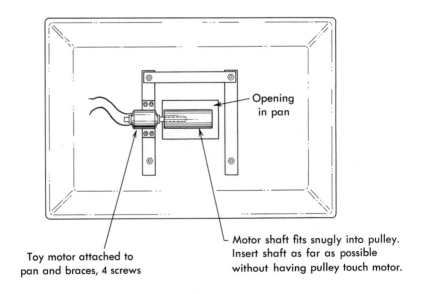

Opening in pan

Toy motor attached to pan and braces, 4 screws

Motor shaft fits snugly into pulley. Insert shaft as far as possible without having pulley touch motor.

Figure 9-14e.   Subassembly B.

line on the pan. In the center of this circle mark off a rectangle about 3 by 2 inches (see Subassembly A, Figure 9-14d) and cut it out with metal shears. Work carefully to avoid jagged edges. Place the rimmed opening of the container over the circle and screw it with four screws set 90° apart to the pan and to the wooden braces on the inside of the pan as shown in Subassembly A.

2. Use four screws to attach the toy motor to the underside of the inverted rectangular pan as shown in Subassembly B (Figure 9-14e). See that the screws pass through the wooden brace. Drill a hole in the center of a broomstick section and force it onto the motor shaft as far as possible without having the pulley touch the motor. This should be a thoroughly tight fit. Glue aluminum foil around the cylindrical part of the broomstick section.

3. Cut a hole in the center of one of the round pans, just large enough to permit you to force the juice container into it. The container juts inside the pan $\frac{1}{4}$ or $\frac{1}{2}$ inch.

4. Determine the position of the upper pulley by matching the position of the lower pulley (see Figure 9-14f). Remove the juice container and use two small angle irons bolted to the inside of the pan to carry two nails that are inserted snugly into the upper pulley (second broomstick section). You may either hammer in the nails or drill holes for them. Glue the aluminum foil to the pulley. Lubricate the angle iron holes that carry the nails.

5. Make a continuous belt out of the rubber strip by overlapping and cementing the ends. After the cement has dried, stretch the belt to fit over both pulleys. See Figure 9-14f.

6. Make a double bend in the piece of screening and use four screws to attach it to the pan bottom as shown in Figure 9-14g. The free end of the screen should miss the belt by $\frac{1}{16}''$ to $\frac{1}{8}''$.

7. Use two screws to attach the lamb's wool to the inside of the rectangular pan so that the wool rubs against the rubber belt. See Figure 9-14d and also Figure 9-14g. The photograph in Figure 9-14a shows a piece of screening instead of lamb's wool, but the lamb's wool produces better results.

8. Connect insulated copper wire to the motor. Punch two holes with a thick nail in the side of the rectangular pan. Slide little pieces of rubber or plastic tubing through these holes. Place

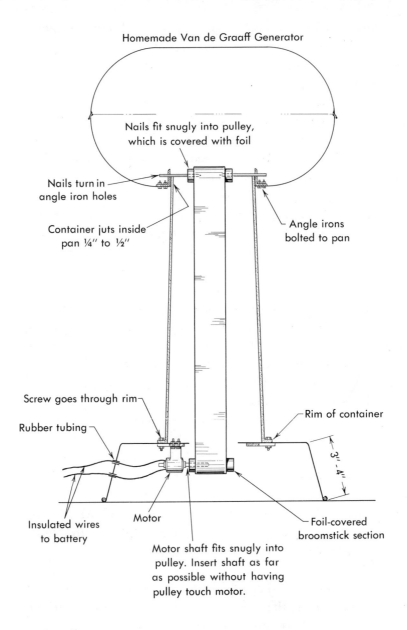

Homemade Van de Graaff Generator

Nails fit snugly into pulley,
which is covered with foil

Nails turn in
angle iron holes

Container juts inside
pan ¼" to ½"

Angle irons
bolted to pan

Screw goes through rim

Rubber tubing

Rim of container

3"- 4"

Insulated wires
to battery

Motor

Foil-covered
broomstick section

Motor shaft fits snugly into
pulley. Insert shaft as far
as possible without having
pulley touch motor.

Figure 9-14f.   View showing pulleys, belt, and motor.

the third pan on top of the upper pan as a cover. The Van de
Graaff is now fully assembled. Connect the insulated wires to one
or two dry cells to set the motor into rotation.

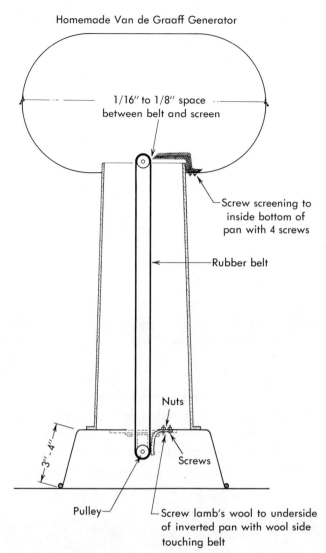

Homemade Van de Graaff Generator

1/16" to 1/8" space
between belt and screen

Screw screening to
inside bottom of
pan with 4 screws

Rubber belt

Nuts

3"–4"

Screws

Pulley

Screw lamb's wool to underside
of inverted pan with wool side
touching belt

Figure 9-14g. View showing wire screen and lamb's wool.

HOW TO USE THE GENERATOR

The charges created by friction of the wool against the rubber belt are picked up by the wire screen, which acts like the "comblike device" mentioned in the description of the real Van de Graaff. The charges collect at the top of the generator and, after a few minutes, cause sparks to appear on the outside. If you bring a

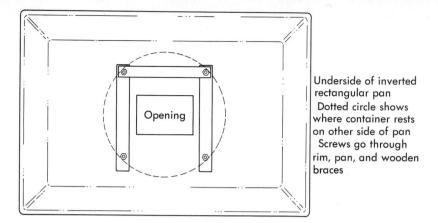

Opening

Underside of inverted rectangular pan
Dotted circle shows where container rests on other side of pan
Screws go through rim, pan, and wooden braces

Figure 9-14h. View showing screws and braces.

metal object within one or two inches of the top of the generator, you can concentrate the voltage and produce a larger spark. A one-inch spark indicates the presence of 50,000 volts. Do not let this figure disturb you. It is quite safe with this generator. However, do not touch the metal object or any part of the generator while it is running or soon after it is shut down, or you will get an uncomfortable shock.

One safe way to bring a metal object near the top of the generator is to place a foil-covered ping-pong or wooden ball at the end of a wooden dowl and hold the other end of the dowel in your hand. Or you can make a stand for the dowel. A fluorescent lamp will glow if it is held on a stand with one end of the tube near the top of the Van de Graaff generator.

CHAPTER 10

RADIOISOTOPES

Radioisotopes is a short way of saying *radioactive isotopes.* Are radioisotopes good or bad? The answer depends upon whether the radioactivity is under control or not. You hear a great deal these days about radioactive fallout and the danger of radioactivity. This is the radioactivity that is not under control. It is the radioactivity that comes from the radioisotopes released into the air from the explosion of test bombs or from the improper disposal of radioactive wastes from nuclear reactors or other nuclear devices. As you know, the fission process creates many different kinds of radioisotopes right in the reactor core itself. Some of these isotopes may find their way into the coolant in the reactor system, if there are leaks. A certain amount of radioactivity is created directly in the coolant when neutrons enter the nuclei of atoms in the impurities that cannot be completely excluded from the water or other coolant.

After a reactor has been in operation for some time, the fissionable material needs to be removed and the uranium or thorium or plutonium needs to be separated from the various isotopes into which the U235 or U233 or plutonium nuclei have disintegrated as the result of fission. These radioisotopes must be carefully kept from contaminating the surrounding area. Some of them can actually be turned to good, controlled use, as we shall point out in some detail in this chapter. Those for which no use is found must be disposed of in some safe manner. There are several kinds of treatment given to the radioactive wastes from reactor operation.

Radioactive wastes may take the form of a gas, a solid, or a liquid. In any case, isotopes with a short half-life are separated from those with a long half-life. The short-lived ones are stored in radiation-proof containers until their radioactivity has ceased. They can then be released into the air or into rivers with no harmful consequences. The long-lived isotopes present a serious problem. They have to be concentrated into the smallest bulk possible and then stored in radiation-proof containers deep in the ground or put into permanent containers and dropped far out in the ocean. This is a problem that has not been completely solved as yet.

Some of the fission products are extracted from the fissionable material and stored for controlled use. For example, strontium 89 and 90, zirconium 95, cesium 137, barium 140, and cerium 141 are some of the fission products that are recovered from the core

Figure 10-1. Working behind the barrier, an operator picks up an isotope storage bottle by means of remote control tongs, viewing the operation in an overhead mirror. (Oak Ridge National Laboratory)

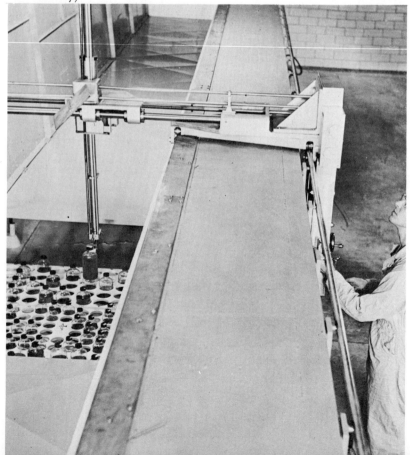

and stored for useful purposes. As time goes on, probably more and more of the fission products can be put to good use.

When we think of radioisotopes as *good,* we think of their controlled use in medicine, agriculture, and industry. Mention has already been made of how radioisotopes are produced by bombardment in an accelerator or by irradiation in a reactor. Also, let us not forget the ones that exist in nature. Therefore, we can see that we have several sources of radioisotopes. In addition, the used reactor fuel itself can serve as a source of gamma radiation. Of these various sources of radioisotopes, the most common is irradiation in a reactor. The Atomic Energy Commission is the largest single supplier of radioisotopes. They are produced in its reactor at Oak Ridge, Tennessee, and then sold wholesale to companies that process them chemically for sale to the users. A great many of the one hundred or so different radioisotopes produced at Oak Ridge are processed and shipped as colorless liquids; others, as invisible gases; some, as pieces of solid metal; and still others, as tiny pills or wafers (Figure 10-1).

Radioisotopes can be used for an amazing variety of useful purposes, from treating some types of cancer to finding out how far a mosquito can fly. Their radioactivity, their ability to send out particles and rays, is the key to their unique usefulness.

RADIOISOTOPES IN MEDICINE

In the medical field, radioisotopes have already proved of great value in diagnosis and research. To a limited extent they are used in the treatment of certain diseases and conditions.

Radioisotopes provide the medical profession with an extremely accurate and reliable tool with which to diagnose illnesses. Because their presence inside the body can be so clearly detected by such instruments as Geiger counters and scintillation counters, they in effect enable the physician to "see" inside the patient and to determine how certain organs and parts of the body are functioning.

The principal method of studying bodily functions is by means of radioactive "tracers." You may know that bells are tied to a few sheep to tell the shepherd where the whole herd is. In the same way, a small amount of radioactive material is added to a substance that is then taken by mouth or injected into the body to show where that substance has settled in the body. A very small amount of radioactive material is sufficient. Even one radioactive atom among a trillion stable ones produces enough radiation to be detected.

The tracer method is used to determine how well certain organs are functioning. For example, suppose the physician wants to find out how a patient's thyroid gland is working. Since the thyroid gland needs iodine for proper functioning, it tends to pick up most of the iodine we get from sea food or from iodized salt. The patient drinks an iodine solution that contains some iodine 131 (half-life — 8 days). Such a drink is sometimes referred to as an "atomic cocktail." The iodine will concentrate in the thyroid gland, taking the radioiodine with it. The amount of radioactivity detected in various parts of the gland tells the physician how the gland is functioning.

The tracer method works well in the diagnosis of circulatory diseases. The normal rate of blood circulation has been determined by the use of sodium 24 (half-life — 15 hours) as a tracer. Now suppose a person shows symptoms of poor circulation of the blood in one leg. Because of the earlier studies of blood circulation, it is known how long it takes the blood to travel from the thigh to the toes and back. Radiosodium in a sodium chloride compound (ordinary salt) is injected into the thigh and then traced with a Geiger counter while the time is noted with a stop watch. If it takes longer than the normal amount of time, then there is evidence that there are obstructions in the blood vessels. In some cases the detector can be used to locate the obstructions.

The rate at which the body consumes oxygen can be measured by means of radioiodine. This measurement, called an iodine uptake test, is more accurate, if more expensive, than the usual basal metabolism that is done with a mechanical device. Since the radioiodine concentrates in the thyroid, the amount of it taken up by the thyroid is an index of how active the thyroid is. The degree of activity of the thyroid is, in turn, a measure of how much oxygen has been consumed.

By using the tracer method, physicians can determine the total blood volume, the total amount of chlorine, sodium, or potassium in the body, the rate of destruction of red blood cells and the presence of pernicious anemia.

The tracer method provides the best way of finding out exactly where a brain tumor is located. A brain tumor is not necessarily a cancer, but any growth inside the brain exerts damaging pressure and must be removed. Normally, substances found in the blood elsewhere in the body are prevented from entering the brain because certain brain cells act as a barrier known as the "blood-brain barrier." In the case of a brain tumor, however, these cells no longer function properly, and substances are able to pass from the bloodstream into the portion of the brain occupied by the tumor. If a radioisotope has been added to a solution that is injected into the bloodstream, some of the radioactive atoms find their way into the tumor but not into the healthy portions of the brain. To locate the tumor, radioisotopes are used that give off gamma rays. The detecting instrument is a scintillation counter connected to a complex recording device. When the gamma rays from the radioactive atoms in the tumor strike the scintillation counter, the recording device tells the physician exactly where the tumor is. He then knows precisely where to operate. If no variation in radiation is detected, the physician then knows that the patient does not have a brain tumor.

In selecting radioisotopes for internal use, it is necessary to use those with short half-lives unless one is sure that the body will soon eliminate them in some way.

Tracers have great value in the study of body chemistry. By labeling or tagging various substances with a radioisotope, the research scientist can follow their progress through the body and determine how the body makes use of them. Most of this work is done with experimental animals. Carbon 14 (half-life — 5600 years) or tritium (half-life — 12.6 years) combined with glucose and taken by mouth shows how glucose is used by the body. Iron 59 (half-life — 46 days) has been used in studies of anemic dogs to find out how the body uses iron in the production of hemoglobin. Since phosphorus is used by the bone marrow in the production of blood cells, phosphorus 32 (half-life — 14 days) will concentrate in the bones. It can therefore be used in the study of the healing process in broken bones by means of radioautographs made during different stages of healing. Radioisotopes are used in studies of how the body uses amino acids, fats, and other nutrients. They are also useful in tracing the absorption of drugs by the body.

The uses of radioisotopes so far described depend upon the fact that their radioactivity can be detected by means of instruments. When radioisotopes are used for the treatment of certain diseases or conditions, it is their destructive power that is put to use — their ability to cause the death of body cells.

For a long time, X-rays produced by high-voltage machines and gamma rays from radium have been used to destroy tissue in the treatment of cancer. To these healing agents have been added several artificially produced radioisotopes, which are used in three ways: at a distance from the body, in contact with the skin, and inside the body.

Cobalt 60 (half-life — 5.3 years) and cesium 137 (half-life — 33 years) are used in the same way as radium. A piece of the radioactive substance is placed at the end of a movable apparatus, and the gamma radiation is directed at the desired portion of the body. By keeping the beam of radiation focused on the malignant tissue while the source revolves around the patient, it is possible to irradiate the cancerous cells more heavily than neighboring healthy tissue, thus destroying the cancerous cells with a minimum of damage to the rest of the body. Radiocobalt can be shaped so that its rays can be focused to penetrate to any desired depth in the body. The movable apparatus used in radiocobalt therapy is called a teletherapy unit because the patient is alone in the room while the technician operates the apparatus from another room, shielded by a thick lead wall (Figure 10-2). He observes the patient through a special type of window that keeps out stray gamma rays.

Since the energy of the gamma rays from radiocobalt is greater than the energy of the gamma rays from radium, radiocobalt radiation is more penetrating than radium radiation. It is also considerably cheaper to use radiocobalt than radium. Two hundred dollars' worth of it is the equivalent of $20,000 worth of radium. Radiocesium is also cheaper than radium, but because of its relatively weak radiation, it is used for shallow therapy.

For the treatment of skin cancer, a thread or thin wire containing radiocobalt is stitched under the skin around the cancer and allowed to remain so that the gamma rays can do their work. When the diseased tissue has been damaged, the thread is removed. Radiocobalt cannot be left in the skin because its comparatively long half-life would make it dangerous to the rest of the body.

In certain types of cancer, a solution of radiogold (Au 198 — half-life — 2.7 days) is injected into the diseased area. It does not cure the cancer, but it can prolong the patient's life by preventing the formation of body fluids harmful to the body.

Because phosphorus concentrates in the bone marrow, where blood cells are manufactured, a radiophosphorus "cocktail" is used in the treatment of a few forms of leukemia, a disease in which too many white blood cells are manufactured, and of polycythemia, a disease in which too many red blood cells are produced. Its beta rays slow down the production of both red and white cells.

You are probably wondering how radiation can destroy cancerous tissue without harming healthy tissue. It so happens that cancer cells are more easily destroyed, partly because they are growing

Figure 10-2. A radiology technician demonstrates the controls of the cobalt therapy unit installed in the Medical Division of the Oak Ridge Institute of Nuclear Studies. The operator may look through the 12-inch thick window, which is filled with lead bromide, a viscous liquid that permits clear vision. (Houston from Oak Ridge Institute of Nuclear Studies)

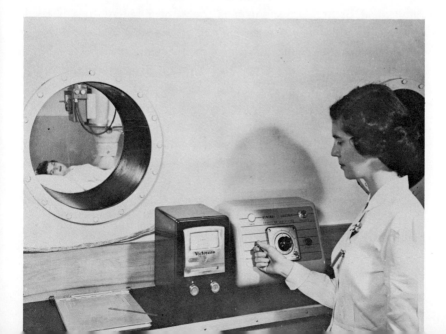

more rapidly. However, radiation also damages healthy cells, but to a lesser degree. There is always a certain risk involved in the use of radiation for therapy.

Sometimes it is desirable to destroy healthy tissue. The destruction of the pituitary gland by means of a proton beam was mentioned earlier. The gland may be destroyed by the implantation of a pellet of yttrium 90 (half-life — 2½ days), which emits beta rays. When the thyroid gland is overactive, it is possible to lower its activity by having the patient drink an atomic cocktail of iodine 131. The iodine goes to the thyroid, where the beta and gamma rays of the radioiodine destroy some of the thyroid cells.

The destructive power of beta rays from strontium 90 (half-life — 24 years) is used to kill off the cells that make up scar tissue. For example, if the cornea of the eye receives a cut, scar tissue forms and interferes with vision. In order to remove this healthy but undesirable tissue, a strontium 90 plaque is used. Since the beta rays do not travel far, they do not injure the eye beyond the scar tissue. The cornea heals with normal transparent tissue in front of the pupil. In the same way, it is possible to remove the extra blood vessels that form on the eye after the cornea has been transplanted.

One special technique, still in the experimental stage, but showing promise, is especially interesting because it involves a nuclear change that is made to take place right inside the body. A patient with a brain tumor receives an injection of boron 10, which circulates through the body and gets into the tumorous portion of the brain because of the breakdown of the blood-brain barrier, as mentioned before. This boron is the same element that is used in the construction of reactor control rods and it is used here for the same reason: because it readily captures neutrons. A beam of neutrons coming from a reactor porthole is directed at the brain tumor. As a boron nucleus captures a neutron, it becomes radioactive and shoots out an alpha particle, which, having a short range, destroys only a nearby cell. The lithium nucleus that remains is harmless. This procedure is known as "neutron capture therapy," and the nuclear change that occurs is expressed as follows:

$$_5B^{10} + {}_0n^1 \rightarrow {}_2He^4 + {}_3Li^7$$

Our lives depend upon the miracle performed daily by green plants. What is their secret? How do they take carbon dioxide from the air, and sunlight, water, and minerals from the soil and turn them into life-giving food for earth's creatures? Through the use of radioactive tracers scientists are learning more about this vital process. Besides satisfying the scientists' curiosity, such knowledge is expected to lead to the production of better and more abundant crops.

Studies have been made of how plants use carbon dioxide and water. Carbon 14 (half-life — 5,600 years) mixed with ordinary carbon 12 is burned to produce radioactive carbon dioxide. The plant is then permitted to breathe in the radioactive gas, which is traced through the plant by means of a Geiger counter. Similarly, oxygen 18 is introduced into the water that is fed to the plant and its absorption followed to study the role of the water.

Valuable studies have also been made of the way in which plants use fertilizers. For example, suppose scientists wish to find out how much phosphorus is needed by different parts of a plant. Radiophosphorus is combined with ordinary phosphate fertilizer in varying proportions. The different mixtures are used in different experimental fields. Plants of the same type are grown in all the fields, with one field using ordinary phosphate as a control. The plants are examined at various stages of growth to determine just where the fertilizer has settled and how much of it is being used. One method is to use a Geiger counter. Another is to make radioautographs. The leaves and stems are placed against photographic film, which is in a light-proof container. The areas where the radiophosphorus is concentrated will show up on the film because of the ionizing effect of the beta rays (Figure 10-3).

You can try a radioautograph of this type yourself by standing a stalk of celery (or some fresh lettuce leaves) in a solution of uranium nitrate. You can buy a small quantity of uranium nitrate from a chemical supply house. It dissolves easily in ordinary tap water. An adequate solution is made by dissolving one teaspoon in 20 teaspoons of water. Do not allow the uranium nitrate to enter your mouth, and be sure to throw away whatever container you use for the experiment. Let the celery stalk stand in the solution for 24 hours.

The light yellow color of the uranium nitrate is usually not visible in celery, but you can detect its presence by means of film. Take a piece of film that is covered with light-proof paper. Lay a few celery leaves against the paper covering on the film, using rubber bands or Scotch tape to hold them tightly flat against the film. Put the film and leaves away undisturbed for two weeks. Then develop it according to the directions given in Appendix A. When you develop the film, it should show the pattern of the leaf veins, proving that the uranium nitrate was carried up into the leaves by the water.

Figure 10-3. A radioautograph of a coleus leaf. This picture was "taken" by means of the beta rays emitted by the radioactive phosphorus, which had been taken up by the plant along with ordinary phosphorus. (Brookhaven National Laboratory)

Studies of how plants use other minerals are carried out in the same way as the phosphorus experiment. A radioisotope of the mineral under study is combined with the usual mineral and the absorption in the plant studied by Geiger counter and radioautographs. In this way, for example, it was discovered that not only the roots of plants absorb nitrogen but also the leaves. Information is also being gathered as to which types of fertilizer a plant needs at various stages of growth.

Another way agricultural production can be improved through the use of radioisotopes is by experimentation with new varieties of plants that are created through the process of mutation. In Chapter 4 mention was made of two theories to account for the mutations that have occurred naturally in plants and animals through the passage of the centuries. These mutations might have been caused by cosmic rays or by radiation from radioactive minerals in the ground. For many years it has been known that X-rays can cause changes in fruit flies in such a way that the changes are passed on to following generations. You may recall that in Chapter 4 we said that the mutations were caused by the fact that the radiation knocked off electrons from the atoms of the material in the genes. Using the same principle, scientists have exposed plants to radiation to cause changes that are passed on through the seeds.

At Brookhaven National Laboratory, scientists have been creating new varieties of plants by exposing them to gamma radiation from radiocobalt (Figure 10-4). A slug of cobalt 60, installed underground inside a lead container, can be raised above ground by means of a pulley operated electrically from a safe distance. Plants receive varying amounts of radiation depending upon their distance from the radiocobalt. By this method a superior variety of corn has been developed that is resistant to certain destructive fungi. Mutations induced by radiation have resulted in the creation of rust-resistant varieties of oats and wheat.

Radioisotopes aid agriculture indirectly by being used in the war against destructive insects. Increased knowledge of the life habits of harmful insects leads to more effective use of insecticides. To study the habits of insects, scientists capture a few specimens and dab them with radioactive paint. Then by means of a Geiger

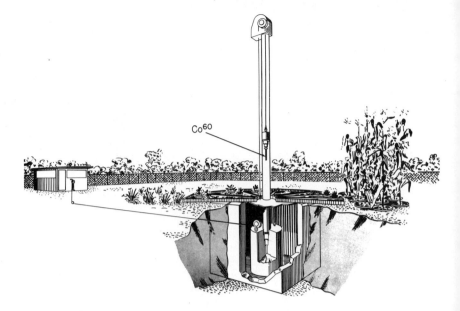

Co⁶⁰

Figure 10-4. Diagram of the installation in the center of the radiation field at Brookhaven National Laboratory, showing underground remote control cable, lead container, cobalt 60 source of gamma rays, and metal pipe housing the source. (Brookhaven National Laboratory)

counter it is possible to trace the path they take through a planted area and to determine which kinds of plants they attack and at what stage of their own growth.

Further useful information is gained by feeding insects radioactive food and tracing its absorption. Material from various organs is extracted and tested for radioactivity by means of a Geiger counter. In this way scientists can learn about the body processes of insects. Such knowledge can be used to make more effective insecticides.

IMPROVING LIVESTOCK

Knowledge of the body processes of animals gained through the use of radioisotopes can help in the production of better livestock. For example, the ability to withstand heat is closely related to the activity of the thyroid gland. Thus, thyroid activity is an excellent

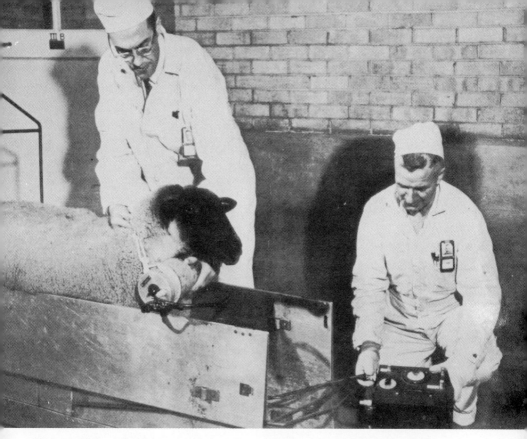

Figure 10-5. A sheep gets its thyroid checked with a Geiger counter to measure the amount of radioiodine it has retained after being fed with radioactivated food. Notice the film badges and pocket dosimeters worn by the technicians. (General Electric, Hanford, Washington)

clue to the way cattle are affected by temperature. By including radioiodine in an animal's diet and measuring its thyroid activity (Figure 10-5), livestock breeders can determine which animals can best withstand heat and can then select these specimens for breeding purposes.

The degree to which various animals can use certain nutrients provides knowledge as to what constitutes the best diet for them. Through the addition of radiosulfur to the sulfur in the diet of chickens and the study of how the sulfur was used by the body, it was learned that chickens can use inorganic sulfur in their body chemistry and that the addition of sulfate to some poultry rations increased the rate of growth. Similarly, studies using calcium and phosphorus tracers revealed the best proportion in which these nutrients should be included in the diet of chickens in order to stimulate egg laying.

RADIOISOTOPES IN INDUSTRY

Industry is already saving hundreds of millions of dollars a year through the use of radioisotopes. As more and more uses are found and as more companies begin to use isotopes, these savings will continue to grow.

The same tracing technique that is used to diagnose disease in the human body or to study plant processes also has industrial applications. The principle is the same. A radioisotope is added to the material to be traced. For example, oil in underground pipes can be traced this way. The same pipeline is often used to carry different kinds of oil, one right after the other, to a central storage site, where each kind is directed to its own tank by means of valves, which must be switched at the right moment. At one time it was hard to know just where one kind of oil in the pipeline ended and the next began. Sometimes two different kinds of oil got mixed in the same storage tank, which meant that a certain quantity was wasted.

Now a small amount of radioactive material can be put into the pipeline at the point where one type of oil is ending and another type is being put in. Then Geiger counters at the other end of the pipeline can be used to find just where one kind of oil ends and the next kind begins so that the valves can be switched at the right moment. Sorting out the different oils when they reach the end of a pipeline means a large saving in oil and money.

In the same way, leaks in water pipes or other kinds of pipes can be found quickly. If a water pipe, for example, breaks underground, it is no longer necessary to dig up the pipe in an effort to locate the break. Now radioisotopes come to the rescue. The chemical engineer places a harmless radioisotope such as phosphorus or iodine into the water at its source. Using a sensitive Geiger counter above ground, he traces the pipeline to the point where the counts suddenly increase or stop. This is the point of the break. If the water is piling up underground in a pool, the count will increase. If it is simply draining off underground, the count will stop. Since the exact spot of the break is thus indicated, very little digging has to be done, at a great saving in time and money, particularly when the pipe is buried in concrete.

This method is very useful in determining whether sewage is entering a water supply. In such a case, the radioactive material is added to the sewage, and the water reservoir is then tested for radioactivity.

An important application of radioisotopes in industry is their use in measurement. What is the level of a liquid in a storage tank? How thick is a sheet of paper or of steel? How much metal has worn off an engine or how much rubber has worn off a tire? The use of radioisotopes can supply the answers.

Where tanks contain dangerous chemicals and it is difficult to measure the level, it is possible to do so by means of a float containing a radioisotope. In the top of the tank there is a Geiger counter that registers the counts on a control panel at a distance from the tank. Instead of registering counts per minute, the dial registers gallons of liquid. The higher the level of the liquid, the higher the number of counts.

Factories often receive orders for sheets of paper, plastic, glass, or metal of a specific uniform thickness. Any variation in thickness, even a thousandth of an inch, will not be acceptable. Radioisotopes provide the most accurate way of measuring the thickness of the material. Let us take as an example the measurement of the sheet steel that forms the body of the familiar tin can. The tin is merely a layer about one thousandth of an inch thick on the thin steel wall of the can. This thin sheet of steel was formed from a huge 10-ton ingot of steel by being pressed between powerful rollers. At one time the thickness of the metal was measured by a micrometer. It was impossible to inspect every sheet while it was being rolled. Machinery had to be stopped. Today, the thickness of the steel sheets is measured continuously while the roller is operating. The method is simple and automatic. All that is needed is a Geiger counter and a radioisotope that gives off gamma rays. As you can see in Figure 10-6, the sheet steel passes over a Geiger counter as it runs out of the rolling mill. Above the sheet steel you can see a lead box containing the radioisotope.

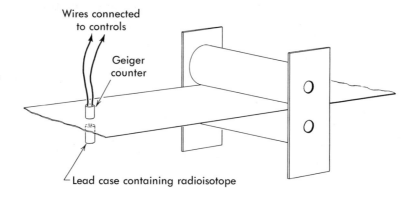

Wires connected
to controls

Geiger
counter

Lead case containing radioisotope

Figure 10-6.   Controlling thickness of sheet metal by means of a radioisotope.

Only the bottom of the box is open. If the steel is of the correct thickness, it will permit the passage of a certain amount of gamma rays, which will be recorded by the counter. If the steel is too thick, the count will go down; if it is too thin, the count will go up. When the steel is coming through with the wrong thickness, the Geiger counter mechanism sends an automatic message to the control room and the rollers are automatically adjusted to produce the correct thickness.

The same principle is followed in measuring the thickness of paper, except that in this case the isotope used emits beta particles. Gamma rays would be too powerful to register enough variation.

Radiation provides an accurate way of determining the density of a material, that is, how tightly or how loosely the material is packed. Before selecting a site for the construction of aircraft runways, highway roadbeds, or waterway dams, it is important to know how solid the ground is. For this purpose a density gauge is used. In one type of density gauge, a steel tube one inch in diameter is driven into the ground. Gamma rays from a cobalt 60 source in the tip of the tube bombard the soil surrounding the tube and are scattered by it. Some radiation returns to a Geiger counter mounted in the top of the tube. The amount of reflected radiation can be translated directly into soil density in weight per cubic unit. More tightly packed soil reflects more radiation.

In the measurement of cigarette density, the amount of radiation that passes through the cigarette to the Geiger counter indicates the firmness of the cigarette. A loosely packed cigarette permits more radiation to get through than a tightly packed one.

No other method is as effective in measuring the amount of wear caused by friction as radioisotopes. Radioisotopes can be used, for instance, in determining exactly how much wear has occurred in engine parts or in tires. Also, the value of the various lubricants in preventing wear can be similarly determined.

Let us start with a typical research project on the wear caused by friction on the walls of the cylinders of an engine. Such a study is made for two purposes: to test different alloys to see which wears best, and to find out which kind of lubricating oil is most effective in preventing wear. In order to determine the amount of wear in the case of a standard automobile engine, which is made of iron, the engine walls are coated with a layer of iron that contains a definite percentage of radioiron. After the engine has been in operation for a certain length of time and some of the iron particles have been worn away and deposited in the lubricating oil, the amount of radioactivity in the oil is measured. By using different alloys and the same kind of oil and running the test engines for the same amount of time, it is possible to tell, by comparing the radioactivity level of the oil in each case, which alloy wears best. Similarly, by using the same alloy but varying the oil, engineers can determine which oil is most effective in reducing the amount of wear in the metal alloy.

The same procedure is used to test wear on piston rings. In this case, the piston rings contain the radioiron.

The same principle is used in testing the wearing quality of different kinds of synthetic rubber or of mixtures of rubber in tires. Since these are made with a large percentage of carbon black in addition to the rubber, radiocarbon is included in the manufacture of the test tires. First the amount of beta particles given off by the carbon 14 is measured before the tires are used. Then the measurement is made after every 1,000 miles of use. The counter will register fewer counts as the tire becomes thinner. Extremely accurate measurements can be made this way. As a matter of fact, the wear can be measured after as little as ten miles of use. Ordinarily, this slight amount of wear cannot be detected with a micrometer.

The use of radioisotopes for purposes of measurement has an interesting application in the detergent industry. Cloth samples are soiled with dirt that contains a radioactive isotope. Then the samples are washed with the various detergents to be tested. The less radioactivity measured after the washing, the more effective the detergent. The same procedure can be used to test the efficiency of washers by using a single type of detergent but different types of washers.

You have already read about the use of gamma rays from radium to determine by means of a radioautograph whether there are any microscopic cracks in metal castings, as in the case of Professor Piccard's diving chamber. Today, gamma rays from radiocobalt and other radioisotopes are used for such purposes. This method, less expensive than the use of radium or X-rays, is used to check on the construction of heavy metal objects such as automobile and airplane engines and to test the welding in the construction of buildings.

RADIOISOTOPES FOR ELEVATORS

One interesting application of radioisotopes is in making elevators stop exactly at floor level. There is a Geiger counter in the floor of the elevator car. At each landing there is a small amount of a radioisotope. The car comes to a stop at each floor when the Geiger counter is exactly in line with the isotope. When the floor of the elevator is exactly flush with the floor of the landing, the Geiger counter picks up the maximum amount of radiation from the isotope. This amount of radiation is needed to operate the control that automatically shuts off the power and puts on the brakes. When the elevator operator pushes a button to go to the next floor, the Geiger counter is disconnected until the car approaches the next floor.

THE ATOMIC BATTERY

In 1959 the United States announced the development of the world's first atomic battery. The source of the power was an alpha-emitting, naturally radioactive isotope — polonium 210 (half-life — 140 days). This was purely an experimental model, costing $30,000 for the polonium alone. Weighing four pounds, it contained enough polonium to provide power for 280 days. It would take 160 pounds of zinc-silver cells to supply the same amount of electrical energy.

This battery operates on two principles. One is that the kinetic energy of the alpha particles is transformed into heat. The other is that an electric current will be generated in a closed circuit of two unlike materials if at the junction point the two materials are at different temperatures. Such a joint is known as a thermocouple.

Another type of atomic battery, called the semiconductor battery, takes advantage of the electron-multiplication principle. High-energy beta particles from strontium 90 bombard a small silicon junction and cause electrons to be ejected and thus create a current.

Atomic batteries would be useful for satellites, for navigation, for giving power to buoys, beacons, remote telephone relays, and automatic weather stations. It has been suggested that radioactive wastes from reactors be used for the production of low-power batteries.

FOOD PRESERVATION

The destructive power of gamma rays has been turned against the insects and bacteria that cause food to spoil. Since 1953 the United States Army has been experimenting with food irradiation. It would greatly simplify the food supply problem of the armed forces if uncanned food could be stored without refrigeration. Irradiation can keep meat from spoiling, potatoes from sprouting (Figure 10-7), and wheat from germinating for long periods of time.

In the Army's irradiation studies the principal sources of radiation are gamma ray emitters, such as cobalt 60, and linear accelerators producing high-speed electrons. Both types of irradiation destroy bacteria by means of ionization: electrons are dislodged from the atoms in the cells of the living creatures. The food to be irradiated is placed in the path of the rays. Since an electron beam

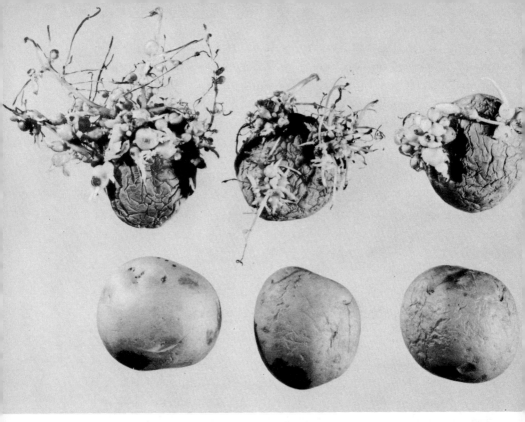

Figure 10-7. Potatoes photographed 16 months after exposure to gamma rays. The one at upper left was not exposed at all; it sprouted and became soft in normal fashion. The other five received varying amounts of radiation. (Brookhaven National Laboratory)

hits only a small spot at one time, it is necessary either to make it scan the object being exposed by directing the beam back and forth and up and down until the entire surface is irradiated or else to diffuse the beam, making it fan out for broader coverage.

The gamma rays pass through the food and are absorbed in the shielding. The energy of the electrons is used up near the surface of the food. The depth to which the electrons penetrate depends upon their energy. For example, 1-Mev electrons penetrate about one-eighth of an inch; 24-Mev electrons penetrate about three inches. Thus, gamma irradiation is used for complete sterilization of food — all bacteria within it are killed off — and electron irradiation is used for killing bacteria on and near the surface.

Completely sterilized food lasts longer than surface-irradiated food, but the latter has a considerably longer shelf-life than non-irradiated food.

There is no doubt as to the effectiveness of radiation in killing off the insects and bacteria that cause food spoilage. There remain the problems of taste and safety. Irradiation frequently changes the flavor of a food, different types of food reacting in different ways. Research continues with the goal of making irradiated food as tasty as possible.

Is irradiated food safe to eat? A large part of the research program is devoted to finding a conclusive answer to this question. One would naturally wonder whether the food itself becomes radioactive. So far, Army spokesmen say that it does not. But there is another factor under careful study. The gamma rays and electrons that kill bacteria by means of ionization also knock electrons off the atoms in the food itself. These released electrons then attach themselves to other atoms, creating new compounds. This is the cause of the change in taste. In addition, these new compounds may in some cases be harmful. To study the possible harmful effects of these new compounds, Army scientists have been feeding irradiated food to 250,000 animals — mice, rats, chickens, dogs, and monkeys — and closely watching their health. Many of these animals are sacrificed after three years and their bodies examined for signs of illness or abnormality. People have also eaten irradiated food, so far with no apparent ill effects. If irradiated food passes the three-year test to the satisfaction of the Food and Drug Administration, it may then be approved for consumption by the public.

CHAPTER 11

A CLOSER LOOK AT THE ATOM

The varied uses of radioisotopes in medicine, agriculture, and industry, the expanding use of nuclear power for electricity and for propulsion, the growing importance of atomic energy in the military field — all these show how quickly man has plunged into the nuclear age. And yet we are really only at its threshold. Who knows what further tremendous developments will take place in this field in your lifetime?

Along with practical developments has come increased knowledge of the nucleus itself. The picture of the atom given in the first chapter of this book is a basic but incomplete one.

What is the atom *really* like? No one can give a complete answer to this question. For years physicists have been patiently examining the atom as well as they can examine something so very small with the tools available. They have been bombarding nuclei with subatomic particles and even such particles themselves in the hope of finding out the true nature of the atom in all its mysterious aspects. They have been theorizing, working out elaborate mathematical equations, trying to reconcile contradictory evidence. They still do not know everything they would like to know, but they have come to a few conclusions. This more detailed and somewhat more exact picture of the atom has not been necessary to an understanding of the material in this book, and physicists writing nontechnically about the atom today still use the simplified picture that was given in the first chapter — the picture of electrons orbiting in various shells around a nucleus made up of protons and neutrons.

To get a fuller, truer picture of the atom, however, we must re-examine the distinction we have been making between particles of matter, such as protons and electrons on the one hand, and electromagnetic radiation, such as X-rays and gamma rays on the other. We think of particles as having mass or weight, of moving through space in the way a bullet or a marble moves, of affecting the motion of other bits of matter when they bump into them. We think of X-rays and gamma rays as light rays, having wave lengths, but no weight or mass. These distinctions are not entirely true. The fact is that light energy has certain characteristics of matter, and particles have certain characteristics of light waves. Let us now see which characteristics are common to both.

PARTICLES OR WAVES?

One striking and difficult point to accept is the fact that, like light, particles have a wave length. When they are moving fast, their wave length is short. When they are moving slowly, their wave length is long. When particles are moving fast and have a short wave length, it is convenient to think of them as bits of matter, as we have been doing throughout this book. When they are moving very slowly, it is more convenient to think of them as radiation in the form of waves. In order to make this point clearer and somewhat more believable, let us consider some facts about the neutron.

We have frequently mentioned fast and slow neutrons. Fast neutrons are those that are kicked out of nuclei. These travel at speeds of about 10,000 miles per second and have energies of about 2 Mev. Slow neutrons are those that have been slowed down by means of a moderator until they have energies of less than one-tenth of an electron volt (.1 ev) and speeds under one mile per second. These are not the true extremes for the neutron. It is estimated that when the neutron is inside the nucleus it has energies of 50 Mev and is moving at extremely high speeds, which are difficult to calculate.

Until now we have said nothing about the movement of the

neutrons inside the nucleus. We have given the impression that a stable nucleus is a quiet, fixed collection of protons and neutrons. In a later section of this chapter we will discuss the movement of protons and neutrons inside the nucleus. When we get into the world of matter that lies beyond our senses, we begin to realize that *nothing* is at rest!

The neutrons inside the nucleus, then, are the fastest neutrons there are. They would also have to be the ones with the smallest wave lengths. And in order to be consistent with the size of the nucleus, their wave length would have to be smaller than the diameter of the nucleus itself. This has been estimated to be 10^{-12} cm, and the wave length of the neutron has been estimated to be 10^{-18} cm.

Now, let us go to the other extreme, to the very slowest neutrons that have so far been observed. We have been talking about the slow neutrons that are found during the operation of a reactor, having been slowed down by the moderator. But physicists have found ways of slowing them still further. They permit a beam of slow neutrons coming from the reactor to pass through a further moderating material and then, in addition, they select from this beam the very slowest neutrons by having the beam pass through a device called a "neutron chopper." These very slow neutrons are called "cold" neutrons. (Fast movement of particles creates heat; therefore slow ones are "cooler.") These cold neutrons move comparatively slowly, at energies of .02 electron volts. At these speeds, their wave lengths are larger — about 2×10^{-8} cm. With wave lengths this large, neutrons behave more like light than like matter. They have been observed to bend as they pass from one material to another. You have seen light rays bend as they pass from air to water. Put a spoon in a glass of water and look at it with your eyes on a level with the top of the water. The spoon will appear to be bent. Neutrons have also been observed to be reflected from a highly polished, mirror-like surface. By *observed* we mean that their presence has been detected through their secondary reactions or decay particles — protons, electrons, and neutrinos.

Electrons also have a wave length, and it too becomes smaller as their speed increases. The way the high-speed electrons bounce off a nucleus reveals something about the structure of the nucleus. If the wave lengths of the electrons were larger than the diameter of the nucleus, the way they bounce off would not reveal anything. Similarly, the electron microscope is used to reveal the structure of plant and animal cells that the ordinary microscope cannot distinguish because the wave length of the electrons is smaller than the wave length of light. An optical (light) microscope reaches its limit when the size of things we look at is about the wave length of light.

If we try to look through an optical microscope at two points that are closer together than one wave length of light, the images of these two points will merge into one, and we will not be able to see them as separate points at all. The wave length of visible light is 4,000 to 7,500 angstroms (see chart of wave lengths on p. 37). The wave length of a 10,000-volt electron is 0.1 angstroms. Although electrons in an electron microscope function as particles of matter, as they do in particle accelerators, nevertheless they could not be used in such a microscope if their wave lengths were not considerably smaller than the wave length of light. In an electron microscope electron beams are directed at the specimen to be seen and photographed. The electrons pass through the thin parts of the specimen but are stopped or deflected by the thick parts. The beam that comes through the specimen carries the pattern of the specimen. The pattern is magnified as the beam passes through several electric and magnetic fields, and the enlarged image appears on a fluorescent screen. The microscope includes photographic equipment to take pictures of the images.

WAVES OR PARTICLES?

Now that we have seen that particles have wave lengths, it should not surprise us to learn that gamma rays and X-rays, in fact, light rays in general, sometimes behave like particles! For example, a gamma ray can knock an electron out of an atom, just as if it were a bit of matter bumping into another bit of matter. This is ionization, and we have already mentioned the fact that gamma rays can produce ions.

This effect occurs in the case of ordinary light rays too. For example, streams of electrons pour from the surface of some metals when a strong beam of light shines on it, as in a solar battery or an electric eye. The light rays actually knock electrons out of the atoms of the metal, just as gamma rays do. This could happen only if the light energy of the beam were concentrated at specific points. These specific points in beams of light are the equivalent of particles. They are thought of as packets or bundles of energy called *quanta* from a form of the Latin word meaning *how much?* You may have heard of the "quantum theory." This is a well-established theory that holds that light energy does not travel in continuous waves but rather in separate bundles of energy. One quantum of radiant energy is known as a photon.

An experiment devised by Professor Jerrold R. Zacharias of the Massachusetts Institute of Technology shows how a beam of light can make a strip of aluminum foil in a high vacuum move in response to the pressure exerted upon it by the photons that make up the beam of light.

In a vacuum tube a tiny strip of aluminum foil (about half an inch square) is suspended from a very delicate quartz fiber, as shown in the diagram in Figure 11-1. A beam of light from a small spotlight is focused first on the right-hand side of the foil, marked B. This pressure makes side B of the foil move slightly away from us and brings side A toward us. As the foil begins to return to its original position, with side B coming toward us, the beam of light is focused on the left-hand side of the foil, marked A. This pressure on side A causes side A to move away from us and reinforces the movement of side B toward us.

The fact that photons can, under certain circumstances, impart kinetic energy to an object, may some day lead to a rather startling application. Scientists are already theorizing about the possibility of what they call "solar sailing." They envision a spaceship in the form of a kind of sailboat, with a huge sail. The sail would receive enough push from the photons in sunlight to be propelled through space. The tails of comets always point away from the sun because of the pressure exerted upon them by photons from the sun.

THE RESTLESS WORLD OF INNER SPACE

If you wanted to portray the movement of all the particles in the

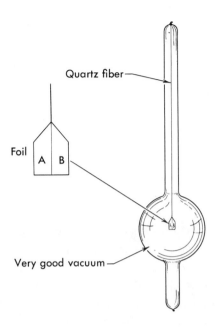

Quartz fiber

Foil

A B

Very good vacuum

Figure 11-1. Diagram of experiment showing that a beam of light can exert enough pressure to move a small piece of aluminum foil suspended by a quartz fiber in a vacuum.

atom by means of a moving model, what a blur of movement would result! Not that physicists have yet acquired a sufficiently clear understanding of these complex movements to form the basis for an exact model. But we can take the approximation that they now offer and try to make such a model in our minds.

You have already pictured the electrons orbiting around the nucleus in different shells. To this motion, add the rotation of each electron on its own axis. This rotation or "spin," as it is called, makes of each electron a tiny magnet.

Now let us try to set the protons and neutrons into their distinctive type of motion. But first we must add something to our concept of what protons and neutrons are. Physicists now regard them as two charged states of the same particle. It is now believed that they freely change places with each other by means of a negative meson that passes between them. As you know, the neutron is slightly heavier than the proton. This difference is explained by the presence of the negative meson, which is thought of as spinning around a positive core in the neutron. Thus the meson is now regarded as the "glue" that holds the nucleus together. When a meson shifts over from a neutron to a proton, the proton becomes a neutron and the neutron becomes a proton. Since these two particles are considered to be two states of the same particle, they are both called nucleons.

Nucleons are now pictured as spinning on their axes and moving around one another. Nucleons that are spinning in the same direction have a stronger attraction for each other than those that are spinning in opposite directions.

The nature of the forces that attract nucleons to one another and therefore hold the nucleus together is not known. Physicists do know, however, that these forces are 35 times as strong as the electrical forces with which we are familiar. They have discovered also that these nuclear forces are strongest when the distance between two nucleons is about one fermi (10^{-13} cm.). When the distance between two nucleons is less than .7 of a fermi, they *repel* each other. When two nucleons are more than a few fermis apart, the nuclear forces have no appreciable effect (Figure 11-2). Nuclear forces operating between two protons have the same strength as those operating between two neutrons. The same seems to be true of the proton-neutron relationship, but the evidence is not yet conclusive.

BETA DECAY

You read earlier that in the case of disintegrating nuclei, sometimes a nucleus becomes the nucleus of an element one step higher in the Periodic Table because a beta particle (electron) has been emitted and a neutron has changed into a proton. It is now fairly well accepted that the electron was not inside the neutron but was created at the time of disintegration. The reason for this statement is that the wave length of the electron is longer than the wave length of the neutron and so it could not possibly fit inside.

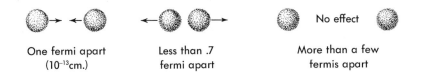

One fermi apart
(10⁻¹³cm.)

Less than .7
fermi apart

More than a few
fermis apart

Figure 11-2. Nuclear forces vary in strength according to the distance between nucleons.

BINDING ENERGY

Although the nature of the force that holds the nucleus together is but dimly guessed at, physicists can calculate very precisely how much energy is represented by this force. They can tell you quite exactly how much energy it takes to hold a certain nucleus together and therefore how much energy it takes to break it up. This energy is called binding energy. It is possible to calculate it in terms of Mev's because mass and energy are interchangeable and the masses of atoms are precisely known.

We are accustomed to think of the whole as being equal to the sum of its parts. For example, if you cut up an apple and weigh it on a delicate scale, the parts will weigh what the uncut apple weighed. But this is *not* true of an atomic nucleus! If you add up the masses of the individual protons and neutrons, you will find that this total is *greater* than the mass of the nucleus as a whole. The apple pieces weigh more than the uncut apple! You can verify this yourself by using the figures for the alpha particle, which has an atomic weight of 4.002764. A proton has an atomic weight of 1.007582, and that of the neutron is 1.00893.

Why does a nucleus weigh less than the sum of its parts? The lost mass has taken the form of energy — the binding energy that holds the nucleus together. Since it is known that one atomic mass unit is the equivalent of 931 Mev of energy, to calculate the binding energy of a certain nucleus, all you have to do is to determine the difference in weight between the whole nucleus and the sum of its parts and multiply that figure by approximately 931 Mev.

Physicists are still seeking further knowledge of the nucleus. Now that newer and more powerful accelerators are in operation, perhaps some of the mystery will be explained. So far, nuclear force, the most vital force in our universe, remains an enigma.

APPENDIXES

Note: Dental film used for X-ray pictures is developed in the same way as ordinary film.

In developing film, always remember to remove the paper covering from the film in complete darkness and then to develop the film in darkness.

You may buy developer already mixed in liquid form, or you may buy the powder and mix your own. You will also need fixer or "hypo," which comes in either liquid or powdered form too, and some plain white vinegar.

These three liquids are put into pans big enough to hold the size of film you are using. You may prepare the liquids with the light on and then, once you are ready to uncover the film, work in darkness. The film, after being unwrapped in the dark, is placed in the developer. Allow it to remain the length of time required for the kind of developer you are using. You can get this information from the container in which the developer comes. An error of one or two minutes is not serious. At the end of the developing time, place the film in the white vinegar for twenty seconds. Then put it into the hypo for ten minutes. Then wash the film thoroughly in running water for twenty minutes. When you develop dental film, be sure that the small piece of film does not slip down the drain. Examine the picture and then allow it to dry by hanging it from a spring-type clothespin.

Another method is to use a developing tank. The tank is filled with the three liquids in turn. A special roll-film tank is needed for developing roll film.

Particles smaller than the atom itself are called subatomic or elementary particles. They are classified into four groups: *photon, leptons* (light-weight), *mesons* (medium-weight), and *baryons* (heavy-weight). This table includes antiparticles. Those that are followed by small black dots have been observed. Those in parentheses must be assumed since there is no known way of observing them. The others are expected to be observed when the proper experiments are conducted.

	Particle	Anti-particle	Mass (in Electron Mass Units)
Photon	γ	(γ)	0
Leptons			
Neutrino	ν	$\bar{\nu}$	0
Electron	e^-	e^+ •	1
Muon (Mu-meson)	μ^-	μ^+ •	207
Mesons			
Pion Pi-Mesons	π^+	π^- •	273
Pion	π^0	(π^0) •	264
Kaon K-Mesons	K^+	K^- •	967
Kaon	K^0	$\bar{K}^0$ •	974
Baryons			
Nucleon (Proton)	p	$\bar{p}$ •	1836
Nucleon (Neutron)	n	$\bar{n}$ •	1838
Lambda–Hyperon	Λ	$\bar{\Lambda}$ •	2182
Sigma–Hyperon	Σ^+	$\bar{\Sigma}^+$	2327
Sigma–Hyperon	Σ^-	$\bar{\Sigma}^-$	2341

Baryons, continued			
Sigma–Hyperon	Σ^0	$\overline{\Sigma}^0$	2332
Xi–Hyperon	Ξ^-	$\overline{\Xi}^-$	2581
Xi–Hyperon	Ξ^0	$\overline{\Xi}^0$	2565

I A								
1.0080 **H** 1 Hydrogen	II A							
6.940 **Li** 3 Lithium	9.013 **Be** 4 Beryllium							
22.991 **Na** 11 Sodium	24.32 **Mg** 12 Magnesium	III B	IV B	V B	VI B	VII B		VIII
39.100 **K** 19 Potassium	40.08 **Ca** 20 Calcium	44.96 **Sc** 21 Scandium	47.90 **Ti** 22 Titanium	50.95 **V** 23 Vanadium	52.01 **Cr** 24 Chromium	54.94 **Mn** 25 Manganese	55.85 **Fe** 26 Iron	58.9 **Co** 27 Cobalt
85.48 **Rb** 37 Rubidium	87.63 **Sr** 38 Strontium	88.92 **Y** 39 Yttrium	91.22 **Zr** 40 Zirconium	92.91 **Nb** 41 Niobium	95.95 **Mo** 42 Molybdenum	(98) **Tc** 43 Technetium	101.1 **Ru** 44 Ruthenium	102.9 **Rh** 45 Rhodium
132.91 **Cs** 55 Cesium	137.36 **Ba** 56 Barium		178.50 **Hf** 72 Hafnium	180.95 **Ta** 73 Tantalum	183.86 **W** 74 Wolfram	186.22 **Re** 75 Rhenium	190.2 **Os** 76 Osmium	192. **Ir** 77 Iridium
(223) **Fr** 87 Francium	(226) **Ra** 88 Radium							

	138.92 **La** 57 Lanthanum	140.13 **Ce** 58 Cerium	140.92 **Pr** 59 Praseodymium	144.27 **Nd** 60 Neodymium	(147) **Pm** 61 Promethium	150.3 **Sm** 62 Samarium
Lanthanide Series						

	(227) **Ac** 89 Actinium	232.05 **Th** 90 Thorium	(231) **Pa** 91 Protactinium	238.07 **U** 92 Uranium	(237) **Np** 93 Neptunium	(242 **Pu** 94 Plutonium
Actinide Series						

Numbers in parentheses are approximate atomic weights.

		III A	IV A	V A	VI A	VII A	
							4.003 **He** 2 Helium
		10.82 **B** 5 Boron	12.011 **C** 6 Carbon	14.008 **N** 7 Nitrogen	16.000 **O** 8 Oxygen	19.00 **F** 9 Fluorine	20.183 **Ne** 10 Neon
I B	II B	26.98 **Al** 13 Aluminum	28.09 **Si** 14 Silicon	30.975 **P** 15 Phosphorus	32.066 **S** 16 Sulfur	35.457 **Cl** 17 Chlorine	39.944 **Ar** 18 Argon
58.71 **Ni** Nickel	63.54 **Cu** 29 Copper	65.38 **Zn** 30 Zinc	69.72 **Ga** 31 Gallium	72.60 **Ge** 32 Germanium	74.91 **As** 33 Arsenic	78.96 **Se** 34 Selenium	79.916 **Br** 35 Bromine	83.80 **Kr** 36 Krypton
106.4 **Pd** Palladium	107.873 **Ag** 47 Silver	112.41 **Cd** 48 Cadmium	114.82 **In** 49 Indium	118.70 **Sn** 50 Tin	121.76 **Sb** 51 Antimony	127.61 **Te** 52 Tellurium	126.91 **I** 53 Iodine	131.30 **Xe** 54 Xenon
195.09 **Pt** Platinum	197.0 **Au** 79 Gold	200.61 **Hg** 80 Mercury	204.39 **Tl** 81 Thallium	207.21 **Pb** 82 Lead	209.00 **Bi** 83 Bismuth	(210) **Po** 84 Polonium	(210) **At** 85 Astatine	(222) **Rn** 86 Radon

152.0 **Eu** Europium	157.26 **Gd** 64 Gadolinium	158.93 **Tb** 65 Terbium	162.51 **Dy** 66 Dyspropium	164.94 **Ho** 67 Holmium	167.27 **Er** 68 Erbium	168.94 **Tm** 69 Thulium	173.04 **Yb** 70 Ytterbium	174.99 **Lu** 71 Lutetium
(243) **Am** Americium	(247) **Cm** 96 Curium	(247) **Bk** 97 Berkelium	(251) **Cf** 98 Californium	(254) **Es** 99 Einsteinium	(253) **Fm** 100 Fermium	(256) **Md** 101 Mendelevium	(254) **No** 102 Nobelium	

Courtesy Central Scientific Company

INDEX

Numbers in italics indicate illustrations.

Krypton, 92, 93

Lambda hyperon, 202
Lead, 44, 46, 47, 49, 54
Lepton, 202
Light
    pressure of, 194, *195*
    wave length of, 37
Linear accelerator, 138, 142-143,
    142, 143
Linear fusion chamber, *131*
Liquid metals
    as coolants, 111, 123
    as reactor core, 110, 122
Liquid sodium cooled reactor,
    123, 125

Magnetic field of plasma, 130,
    131, 134
Magnetic mirror, 132
Mass into energy, 47, 93, 107,
    118, 197
Mass of accelerated particle, 149
Matter, 12
Mechanical energy, 25
Mechanical hands, *114*
Meitner, Lise, 91, 92
Mendelevium, 159
Meson, 57, 156, 158
    in nucleus, 196
Mev, 25
Milk-bottle electroscope,
    29-30, *30*
Moderator, 97, 111, 122, 123, 126
Molecules, 24
Monazite sands, 42
Mu-meson, 202
Muon, 202
Mutations, 46, 179

Nautilus, U.S.S., *124*
Naval Research Laboratory, 102
    reactor, 102, *103, 104,* 108-111,
    115, 116
Neptunium, 105, 158
Neutrino, 45, 202
Neutron balance in reactor, *106*
Neutron beams, 91, 161
Neutron capture, 97
    therapy, 176
Neutron counter, 73, 112
Neutron detector, 95
Neutron emission, *93,* 94, 97
Neutron production in reactor,
    104-106
Neutron-proton reaction, 196
Neutron scattering, 116
Neutron spin, 195
Neutrons, 13, 16, 18, 21, 57,
    89, 103
    "cold," 116, 192
    delayed, 105
    discovery of, 89
    energy of, 105, 191
    "fast," 91, 116, 126
    in fission, 94, 96, 97, 103, 104
    in fusion, 133
    inducing radioactivity, 91
    in reactor, 103, 115, 121
    "slow," 91
    uses of, 113-116
    wave, nature of, 191
Nitrogen disintegration by
    cosmic rays, 59
Nobelium, 159
Notation, atomic, 17
Nuclear energy release, 118-119
Nuclear explosions, 126
Nuclear film emulsion, *60,* 61,
    160

Proton synchrotron, 137, 138,
150-152

Quanta, 194
Quantum theory, 194
"Quenched" current, 74

Radiant energy, 25
Radiation, 42
    danger sign, *115*
    density measure by, 184
    harmful, 97
    of plants, 179, *180*
    protection, 52
    study of effects of, 161
    therapy, 174
Radioactive atoms, 42
Radioactive ores
    experiments with, 51-52, 80,
        99-101
    identification of, 51-52
Radioactive radiation
    absorption, *46*
Radioactive wastes, 170
Radioactivity, 41-42
    artificial, 89, 154
    as source of energy, 47
Radioautograph
    Fiesta Ware, 50, *51*
    plant, 177, 178
    radioactive ore, 51-52
    radium watch dial, 41
    thorium mantle, *49,* 49-50
Radiocarbon, 42
    dating, 59
    and tire wear, 185-186
Radiocobalt, 174-175
    plant irradiation by, 179, *180*
    therapy, 174

Radiogold, 175
Radioiodine
    "cocktail," 172
    and sheep thyroid, 180,
        181, *181*
Radioisotopes, 169-186
    in agriculture, 177-179
    and automobiles, 185
    and detergents, 186
    and elevators, 186
    in industry, 182-186
    and insects, 179-180
    and liquid levels, 183
    and livestock, 180-181
    in medicine, 171-176
    production of, 112, *113*
    and thickness control, 183-184,
        184
Radiophosphorus
    in bones, 173
    "cocktail," 175
    in fertilizer studies, 177
Radiosodium and circulatory
    diseases, 172
Radiostrontium and the eye, 176
Radiosulfur and animals, 181
Radium, 41, 42, 43, 44, 174
    decay, *44*
    half-life, 48, *48*
Radium ore, 42
Radon-beryllium, 91
Rays, table of characteristics of,
    47
Reactor
    construction, 107-109
    cooling agent, 110, 111, 122
    core, 96, 108-110, 120,
        122-123

Triton, 17, 128-129
Triton, U.S.S., 125
Tritium, 17, 128, 129,.173
TV screen experiments, 32-33,
  39-40

Uranium, 21, 43, 91-95
  half-life, 49
U 233, 110, 123, 169
  source of, 122
U 235, 96, 103, 126, 169
  fission, 92-94, 104
  separation, 109-110
U 238, 159
  decay to plutonium, 105-106
Uranium core, 103, 108, 109,
  120, 122, 123
Uranium fission, 103-104.
  See also Fission
Uranium hexafluoride, 110
Uranium nucleus, 92-94
Uranium ore, 42, 95
  in Geiger counter experi-
    ment, 80
  radioautograph, 51-52
Uranium oxide, 50
  fuel, 95, 121

Van de Graaff generator, 137,
  140-141, *141*, 152
  homemade, 161-168, *162,
    163, 164, 166, 167, 168*
Volt, 25

Water
  composition of, 24
  used as moderator, 91, 111

Xi-hyperon, 203
X-ray (s), 36, 136, 160, 193
  absorption, 39
  body absorption, 38
  crystallography, 39
  dental, 40
  diffraction, 116
  effect on film, 38
  film development, 40
  ionizing effect on tissue, 46
  and magnetic field, 45
  pictures, 39-40
  speed, 37-38
  on TV screen, 40

Z number, 20
Zacharias, Jerrold R., 194
Zinc sulfide screen, 82, 86
Zirconium, 120, 123